"Wisely written and carefully constructed–this book will provide much needed help and inspiration for creating or improving love relationships. Use these positive ideas!"
—Rev. Robert Schuller
Pastor and host of THE HOUR OF POWER

"Fantastic! This is an extraordinary book that can make any single or married person's life better. Brilliant strategies and practical insights–one of the best relationship books I have ever read."
—Ken Blanchard, Ph.D.,
author of THE ONE MINUTE MANAGER

"This is the best book I've ever read on interpersonal communication and emotional wellness."
—Denis Waitley, Ph.D.,
author of PSYCHOLOGY OF WINNING

"I could not put the book down. Using simple, easy-to-follow exercises, CREATING PEACE & PASSION IN YOUR LOVE RELATIONSHIP genuinely delivers what it promises. It is the best book ever on relationships."
—Natasha Josefowitz, Ph.D.,
author of PATHS TO POWER

"CREATING PEACE & PASSION IN YOUR LOVE RELATIONSHIP provides the exercises that allow us to experience a more loving life with our mate—not just read about it."
—Warren Farrell, Ph.D.,
author of WHY MEN ARE THE WAY THEY ARE

CREATING PEACE & PASSION IN YOUR LOVE RELATIONSHIP presents a revolutionary program for strengthening your love relationship.

New York Times **bestselling author Harold H. Bloomfield, M.D., has created a practical, powerful, easy-to-follow Love Fitness program** that will teach you how to speak the language of intimate feelings, defuse anger, heal hurts and put the passion back in sex and the magic back in love.

Dr. Bloomfield shares his knowledge and insights in this landmark book that details innovative strategies and inspiring success stories. By offering a series of enlightening Love Fitness tests, relationship workouts, and simple exercises that produce remarkable results, he teaches couples the essential skills for a lasting adventure of the heart–a lifetime of loving and being loved. You will:

- Find the key to sharing feelings, desires, sexual needs, even difficult emotions such as fear, hurt and anger, in positive, constructive ways.
- Discover the three magic words that will help you to really connect with one other.
- Learn the secrets of "Heart Talks" to open up intimacy and improve sexual communication.
- Bring romance and passion back into your life and lovemaking.
- Recognize how to heal the resentments and regrets that can tear a relationship apart.
- Explore your "Habits of the Heart"–the assumptions that determine the success of your love relationship.

Whether you are experiencing the intoxicating optimism of a new romance, the troubling uncertainties of a mature partnership, or something in between, you will find this provocative, groundbreaking program offers new hope to anyone wishing to move toward greater commitment, intimacy and passion.

Creating
Peace & Passion
In Your
Love
Relationship

Harold H.
Bloomfield, M.D.

Afterword by Rev. Dr. Janine H. Burns

Peace Publishing

Peace Publishing
2412 Green Hills Way
Vista, CA 92084

Dr. Bloomfield is a Master Life Coach
and Love Relationship Counselor.
To schedule a private phone consultation,
please call (858) 635-1235.

Library of Congress Catologing-in-Publication Data

Bloomfield, Harold H., 1944-
Formerly titled Lifemates: the love fitness program for a lasting relationship
by Harold H. Bloomfield, M.D. and
Sirah Vettese, Ph.D. with Robert B. Kory

p.   cm.
ISBN
1. Love.   2. Intimacy (Psychology)   3. Interpersonal
communication. 4. Interpersonal relations.

BF575,L8B57   1989
158'.24-dc19   88-28577
CIP
First Printing, March, 1989
Completely revised Edition July 2004

1 2 3 4 5 6 7 8 9

**Dedicated to Shazara
and to all creating peace and passion.**

Contents

Chapter 1

Love Fitness

TO CREATE PEACE AND PASSION IN YOUR LOVE relationship, you must communicate heart-to-heart. Yet few people realize how out of shape they are when it comes to intimate communication and, therefore, their ability to love and be loved. Most of us are afraid of letting others know who we really are and what we really feel, and yet we expect that a great relationship should be easy to achieve.

Couples in terrific relationships often evoke comments such as, "They are so lucky," or "Of course they've got a fantastic relationship, they were made for each other." The implication is that great relationships are found, not created. If you question these couples, however, you will discover their secret to an enduring peaceful and passionate love relationship: open, heart-to-heart communication.

You don't need to be a psychiatrist to diagnose the discouragement and frustration that abound in relationships today. Women feel angry with men who don't really listen and can't share tender feelings. Many men are fearful of self-disclosure and commitment. Couples become exasperated when each tries to understand what the other actually wants.

Too many relationships start out with stars-and-rockets only to fizzle out in boredom and resentment. Partners once in love give up on each other, through either resignation or divorce. The chief cause of this epidemic of failed relationships is the inability to share deep feelings and experience emotional intimacy.

For love to grow there must be a solid foundation of safety and trust. You must be able to share your intimate thoughts and feelings without fear of being ridiculed or rejected. You have to be able to share with your partner what's on your mind without the fear of being humiliated or embarrassed.

Communication problems in most relationships stem from poor emotional habits, learned in childhood from parents and other role models. We each carry in our memories a backlog of painful, if not traumatic, experiences. These are the times in past love relationships when we felt belittled, ignored, abandoned, attacked, rejected or betrayed.

We recreate these past traumas in our current relationships with what Freud called the "repetition compulsion." We may try to forget or avoid these painful emotions, but suppressed feelings resurface, sometimes with a vengeance: "What you resist, persists." What was once a close passionate relationship begins to suffer.

A diminished passion or lower libido can be due to a whole host of psychological problems (e.g., depression, grief, low self-esteem, poor body image); biological factors (e.g., diabetes, alcoholism, menopause, male climacteric); medications (e.g., hypertensive medications, antidepressants, pain pills); and relationship issues (e.g., resentment, jealousy, unresolved hurt and anger). This book deals primarily with the latter.

Most people are accustomed to treating problems in their relationships with emotional Band-Aids. Partners stuck in these painful negative patterns become frustrated. One or both holds back anger, which may resemble a seething volcano. Resentment develops, sex goes flat, and blaming and criticizing

2

become predominant.

Typically, couples avoid facing problems in their relationships for the same reason they avoid sharing deep feelings–fear. The emotional cost of sharing raw feelings seems way too high when you lack the proper communication skills. You may feel overwhelmed with emotions of anger, hurt and jealousy. With each failure of communication, the willingness to try becomes further diminished. You might think, "Why bother?" As intimate communication becomes blocked, so does your love and passion. Sexual boredom or an "I don't care" attitude often sets in. You might feel hopeless and in despair, and think the love relationship is untenable.

"Psychosclerosis":
The Hardening of Emotional Habits

A major concern of modern medicine and physical fitness experts is arteriosclerosis, a hardening of the arteries resulting from poor diet, stress and inadequate exercise. There is a parallel psychological process for which I have coined the term *"psychosclerosis"*–a hardening of the mind, heart and spirit. Just as arteriosclerosis constricts arteries, causing major diseases, psychosclerosis constricts love, thereby limiting self-expression, eroding communication and narrowing the capacity for peace and passion.

The parallels between arteriosclerosis and psychosclerosis are revealing. While arteriosclerosis makes arteries stiff, psychosclerosis makes relationships brittle. Arteriosclerosis takes the joy out of exercise; psychosclerosis takes the passion out of a relationship. The longer arteriosclerosis goes unchecked, the greater the risk of heart attack or stroke. Similarly, the longer psychosclerosis goes unchallenged in a relationship, the greater the chance that love will wither and cause the relationship to end in chronic bitterness, despair or divorce.

Psychosclerosis develops insidiously, and quite predictably, in relationships. At the outset of most relationships, communication is supple and vibrant as couples inevitably go through emotional workouts without the specific intention of doing so. The very process of getting to know someone for the first time challenges your feelings and attitudes; you naturally bend to accommodate and learn about another human being. This process is usually exciting, and if it becomes sufficiently charged with emotional energy, you may feel yourself falling in love.

If the relationship endures, however, emotional habits begin to take over. One person may tend to get irritable easily, so the other becomes excessively accommodating. One may be able to express anger only through the "silent treatment," so the other learns to deal with problems in the relationship through emotional withdrawal. One person may harbor sexual performance anxieties, so the other accepts routine sex to allay these fears. Eventually this system of interlocking emotional habits becomes so rigid that the need for heart-to-heart communication, as well as for self-expression, goes unmet. Anger, resentment and frustration are the inevitable consequences.

To some degree, everyone suffers from psychosclerosis, as do almost all relationships. Consider the following expressions, which hint at psychosclerosis: [1]

"What's the use, he/she will never change . . ."

"I can't get through to him/her. . ."

"Our sex life is boring."

"Nothing ever goes right for us anymore."

"We don't connect like we used to."

"Nobody understands me."

"Is this all there is to love?"

"I don't know what he/she wants."

"Nothing I say makes any difference."

"We never talk about what is really important."

Psychosclerosis destroys relationships in three principal ways. First, it causes resistance to personal growth. Feelings stop flowing and emotional habits can become carved in psychological stone. Second, it can cause you to feel hopeless about improving your relationship. Inflexibility can make you feel defeated before you even try to evoke change. Third, psychosclerosis impairs your ability to listen to your partner, and your partner's ability to listen to you. Given these emotional effects, overcoming psychosclerosis is vital to a peaceful and passionate love relationship.

How much freedom do you have in your emotional responses? Can other people provoke or hurt you easily? Or do you consciously choose your emotional responses for the most effective communication? The first step in overcoming psychosclerosis is recognizing your power to choose the quality of your experience. Don't think this statement is merely a simplistic self-help formula. Obviously, events happen in people's lives over which they have little or no control. Personal tragedy rightfully begets sadness and tears, just as a great success generates energy and joy. My point is, however, that emotional responses need not be automatic.

Behavioral psychologists claim that most human interactions

are governed by automatic, predictable, stimulus-response patterns. Your spouse comes home feeling distressed; you get tense. Your partner gets angry; you feel intimidated. Your partner fails to respond sexually; you feel rejected. These are examples of common stimulus-response patterns in relationships. But these observations don't go far enough. Remember, the behaviorists developed their theories by observing pigeons. There is obviously something more to consider when talking about humans–and that something more is the essential quality of freedom. People have the ability to choose their responses, even during trying emotional circumstances–as long as psychosclerosis has not made their emotional habits entirely automatic and rigid.

Your ability to choose your emotional responses is fundamental to your relationship. Just as you can change your body through diet and exercise, so too, you can change psychosclerotic patterns in your relationships.

Relationship Workouts

Many people are familiar with the rewards of getting in shape, improving their diet and learning to give up destructive habits such as excessive drinking and smoking. The benefits far outweigh the costs required to practice and sustain these new habits. Within a similar framework, you can also develop healthier love relationships.

With the right emotional workouts, you can learn to open up to your partner as never before. You can learn the skills necessary to create a love relationship that lasts. You can enjoy more peace and passion in your relationship through the joys of intimacy.

The Love Fitness Program prevents and reverses the emotional damage that erodes love. The program can help prevent and heal relationship problems, just as a physical fitness program can help prevent and heal disease. I have developed a series of emotional workouts to teach you the communication skills necessary to create a peaceful, passionate love relationship.

When each partner is committed to their personal development, as well as to their growth as a couple, a relationship can flourish. Love alone is not enough, because love can fade in the face of inevitable misunderstandings, small hurts, repressed anger and resentment. In order to create a lasting love relationship, you must become a skillful communicator in the complex language of the heart.

This book provides the strategies, techniques and exercises necessary for your relationship to not only survive, but thrive. You can go beyond making a relationship just "work," to progressively unfolding a spiritual adventure of the heart. When love unfolds to unprecedented depths, it awakens the senses, enlivens passion and opens horizons of spirit.

Love Fitness is not a state you achieve once and for all, any more than physical fitness is everlasting. Rather, it requires an ongoing commitment to personal growth and continued development of your relationship. A lasting love relationship must deal with the inevitable challenges and crises of life–the birth and rearing of children, career successes and failures, illnesses, death of parents or loved ones, children growing up and moving away, and retirement.

All of these events are made sweeter and more manageable by the sharing of love. Yet each of these events presents new challenges to sustaining the heart-to-heart communication that is necessary to keep love vibrantly alive.

There are additional parallels between the Love Fitness Program and physical fitness. The program is primarily intended to develop emotional strength, essential to create and sustain a dynamic love relationship. The emotional workouts described are aimed at assisting each love partner to take 100 percent responsibility for the quality of the relationship. Blaming and complaining don't work!

The Love Fitness Program develops emotional grace, the ability to accept your partner's strengths and limitations. The intense enjoyment of heart-to-heart communication replaces the idealized effort to make your partner into something he or she is not. The program also develops emotional vitality, agility and timing. You learn when to confront and when to hold back; and how to express anger in safe, effective ways.

I use the fitness analogy because it best summarizes both the theoretical approach and the practical benefits of my program. It is based on modern psychological research and time-honored spiritual knowledge.

A revolution has occurred in psychology over the past several decades, equivalent perhaps to the impact of the microchip on the quality of modern living. At the core of this revolution is a progression beyond the old psychoanalytic model, which focuses on resolving past traumas, to the cognitive-behavioral model. The cognitive-behavioral model teaches more effective mental and behavioral skills to replace thoughts and actions that are maladaptive. This approach brings a brighter view of personal growth and spiritual development.

The Love Fitness Program is based on the premise that the best therapist lies within. You are no doubt aware of your body's enormous physical regenerative abilities. Think of the healing energy your body mobilizes to mend a broken bone. That same healing and regenerative capacity exists emotionally. Exercising your emotions has broad beneficial effects similar to exercising your body. When you practice your emotional workouts, you put your capacity for psychological growth into high gear.

A fundamental premise of this program is that no one can change your emotional habits but you. You must first identify the attitudes and beliefs that no longer serve you. You must then choose the corresponding emotional workouts and communication skills to focus on, so love can truly thrive. Ultimately, you and you alone are responsible for your personal growth and the quality of your relationship.

Most people take themselves far too seriously. With a little perspective and humor you can find solutions to relationship problems that may seem insurmountable. The Love Fitness Program is intended to be enjoyable. You should find many of the workouts not only challenging and informative, but also fun and entertaining.

How Emotionally Fit for Love Are You?
Quiz One

The place to begin the Love Fitness Program is with a self-assessment. Testing at the outset of a physical fitness program is helpful in determining your current level of physical fitness and in assessing where you need emphasis. So, too, initial evaluation in the Love Fitness Program is helpful in identifying your current emotional strengths and communication skills.

With the following quiz you will learn how your feelings, attitudes and behaviors affect the quality of your relationship. You will also receive feedback on the specific aspects of Love Fitness you need to focus on the most. Mark each of the following statements true or false:

1. My self-esteem has increased since being in this relationship.
2. I can freely express my need for private time.
3. I seem to confide more in my friends than in my partner.
4. I am not afraid to let my partner see me cry.
5. I sometimes feel bullied or manipulated by my partner.
6. Revealing my innermost feelings is easy for me.

7. When I'm upset, I tend to blame my partner.
8. I feel my partner truly understands and appreciates me.
9. I get upset when my partner criticizes my shortcomings.
10. I tend to be overly critical or short-tempered with my partner.
11. I frequently feel upset or angry about things my partner has said or done.
12. I drink excessively, use drugs or overeat to mask negative feelings.
13. I am supportive of my partner when he/she feels vulnerable and insecure.
14. I compare my partner unfavorably to other mates (less attractive, less sensitive, less successful, etc.).
15. I do not depend on my partner for approval or validation.
16. I feel guilty when my partner feels unhappy, disappointed or hurt.
17. I have forgiven my partner for the times he/she has hurt me.
18. I enjoy passionate lovemaking with my partner.
19. I feel my partner's barriers go up when I'm feeling emotionally vulnerable.
20. I spend too much time and energy "working on" and "fixing" the relationship.
21. I'm always the one arranging an intimate dinner or romantic weekend.
22. I enjoy sharing my sexual fantasies with my partner.
23. My partner and I make all major decisions together.
24. As my relationship continues, I tend to feel bored, disillusioned or trapped.
25. I'm afraid to assert myself because of my partner's temper.
26. I would feel comfortable revealing anything about my past to my partner.
27. It is difficult for me to give criticism to my partner.

28. In a love quarrel, I am inclined to give up in frustration.
29. I don't like to admit it, but sometimes I talk down to or patronize my partner.
30. When differences emerge, I'm afraid of disapproval, abandonment or rejection.
31. I feel comfortable asking my partner for what I truly want and need.
32. My partner is also my best friend, whom I can always count on.

Now go back over the questions and give yourself one point for each true response to questions 1, 2, 4, 6, 8, 13, 15, 17, 18, 22, 23, 26, 31 and 32; give yourself another point for each false response to questions 3, 5, 7, 9, 10, 11, 12, 14, 16, 19, 20, 21, 24, 25, 27, 28, 29 and 30. Add up your score. Here is a summary to help you interpret your results:

25-32   You are enjoying a very high level of Love Fitness. You enjoy loving and being loved, but you're also independent. You are comfortable expressing and receiving intimate feelings.

17-24   Your fitness for love is above average. In some areas, you may be afraid to express your feelings; in others, you may need to be more supportive of your partner. Focus on the corresponding chapters to bring about the changes required to experience greater intimacy and love.

9-16   Your relationship is badly out of shape. Most people score in this range: a fair to poor level of intimate communication. When it comes to Love Fitness, it's as if most of us are on a junk-food diet and have a sedentary, stressful lifestyle. If you've had any experience with the joys of developing physical fitness, you know how rewarding a regular program of physical workouts can be. So, too, when you take the time to practice the exercises in this book, you can discover the joys and rewards of greater fitness for love.

1-8 You're probably feeling a good deal of frustration in your relationship. You have difficulty expressing and accepting intimate feelings. You can experience substantial personal growth by working through the exercises in this book. Consider consulting a psychotherapist or marriage counselor.

How Fit for Love is Your Relationship? Quiz Two

This test is aimed at assessing the Love Fitness of your relationship. In answer to each of the following twenty-five questions, give yourself 1, 2, 3 or 4 points: 1 = rarely; 2 = sometimes; 3 = often; and 4 = usually. If you are not currently in a relationship, answer the questions based on your last significant relationship. In parentheses are the chapters in which these issues are discussed.

1. Are you comfortable listening to your partner's anger? (Chapter 5)
2. Do you accept your partner completely without trying to change him/her? (Chapter 7)
3. When it comes to making major decisions about careers, children and lifestyle, do you feel like an equal partner? (Chapter 7)
4. Are you fearful of being trapped in a committed love relationship or marriage? (Chapter 6)
5. Do you create laughter, fun and play in your lovemaking? (Chapter 4)

6. Are you comfortable saying "no" to your partner? (Chapter 5)

7. Are you at ease letting your partner know when you feel neglected? (Chapter 2)

8. Do you trust your partner's loyalty and sexual fidelity? (Chapter 4)

9. Are you able to express feelings of jealousy without fearing how your partner will react? (Chapter 2)

10. Is your lovemaking tender and exciting? (Chapter 4)

11. Do you have open, intimate conversations with your partner? (Chapter 3)

12. Are you good at receiving criticism from your partner? (Chapter 2)

13. Can you let down your barriers and bare your soul to your partner? (Chapter 3)

14. Can you share your insecurities and failures as openly as your strengths and victories? (Chapter 3)

15. Do you feel free of resentment and bitterness toward your partner? (Chapter 6)

16. Do you resolve your disputes satisfactorily? (Chapter 5)

17. Do you feel that your partner is also a close friend? (Chapter 3)

18. Can you express anger appropriately and constructively? (Chapter 5)

19. At your request, would your partner join you in counseling? (Chapter 6)

20. Have you forgiven your partner for those times when he/she may have hurt you deeply? (Chapter 6)

21. Can you listen receptively to your partner's hurt feelings without becoming defensive? (Chapter 2)

22. Do you respect your partner's work, values and opinions? (Chapter 7)

23. Are you and your partner sexually free, spontaneous and unpredictable? (Chapter 4)

24. Do you feel understood, nurtured and cared for by your partner? (Chapter 2)
25. Do you feel supported in achieving your life goals? (Chapter 7)

Now, add up your score.

80-100 Your relationship is in great shape. You and your partner trust and respect one another. You know how to be both intimate and autonomous. Your emotional exchange is excellent and you are enjoying a high level of Love Fitness.

60-79   Your relationship is in good shape…but why not raise the quality of your relationship to the highest levels of peace and passion?

40-59   Your relationship fitness is below average. It is starting to get flabby and may already be quite out of shape. You may not notice it yet, but there is a significant risk that bigger problems may emerge in your relationship. You basically have two choices: You can put up with a flabby, out-of-shape love relationship and hope that problems don't arise, or you can work to create a higher level of Love Fitness.

20-39   Your relationship is seriously out of shape. You can't count on getting by without making a commitment to improving Love Fitness.

1-19   Your relationship is in crisis. The relationship has deteriorated to the point where it is unlikely that you can solve the problems you face on your own. Find a well-qualified therapist to assist you.

Refer to the chapters in which these issues are discussed. By reviewing those questions answered with a 1 (rarely) or 2 (sometimes), you can see where you need the most exercise and practice, and which chapters deserve your special attention.

Immediately Helpful Tips

There is no greater healing energy than love. It is the candle that dispels the darkness, regardless of how or why the darkness was created. When you are in conflict with your partner, there is a choice: to fight, flee or work through the upheaval to re-connect with love. Here are some valuable Love Fitness tips, to be explored in more detail in later chapters:

1. *Check Your Assumptions.* It's only natural to make assumptions about what your partner is thinking or feeling, but you can easily be wrong. Furthermore, it is unreasonable, and a breach of trust, to contradict what your partner says he or she feels. The solution is simple: Ask what your partner is feeling and accept the report as true. Cultivate your ability to listen well, without interrupting or jumping to conclusions.
2. *Don't Demand Perfection.* Do you have a tendency to overreact at the first sign of upset? Try to remember that with love comes a certain amount of hurt, anger and frustration. When your partner is upset, try to put yourself in his or her place and ask yourself, "Why does he/she feel this way?" "What made him/her behave this way?" "What can I do to convey more love and understanding right now?" Try to use the conflicts that arise as opportunities to learn and grow.
3. *Curb Your Need to Be Right.* Trying to "win" when you and your partner disagree is futile. Fierce competition usually leads to both of you losing, to diminished affection and the tendency of the "loser" to want to get even. Most disagreements have to do with priorities, choices, values

and opinions, for which there are no absolute standards of right or wrong. When you are in a dispute, try to aim for a resolution in which both of you win, both of you are right, and to the greatest extent possible, both of your needs are fulfilled. Learn to accept reasonable criticism without becoming defensive or vengeful. Don't argue, don't attempt to justify your actions, and above all, don't respond immediately and reactively with criticism of your own. The more you resist listening, the more your partner will persist in telling you what you don't want to hear.

4. *Acknowledge and Appreciate.* A relationship thrives on appreciation. The best way to get your partner to acknowledge you more is to appreciate him or her more. Get into the habit of thanking your partner for the small ways he or she makes your life better and express your admiration for those things he or she does well. Focus on the good, and then talk about it. Appreciation is contagious.

5. *Don't Try to Change Your Partner.* You may have entered your relationship hoping that your partner would be everything your previous partners were not. When he or she turns out to have flaws (just like everyone else), you have a choice: acceptance or coercion. With the exception of certain things that are not negotiable, like infidelity, substance abuse and violence, most of the qualities you might be tempted to try to change are probably minor traits you're better off learning to live with. You can certainly make requests, express your preferences and offer feedback, but manipulating your partner into becoming something he or she is not–or does not care to be–is a prescription for resentment.

6. *Take Responsibility for Your Own Happiness.* Many of us enter relationships with the unconscious hope, wish or expectation that our partner will rescue us and make us happy. No matter how committed your relationship is, you will always be single in one important sense: *your*

happiness is your own responsibility. Not even the most devoted and caring partner can solve all your problems, erase all the pain of your past or magically bestow happiness upon you. To give to your partner, you must take care of yourself. Treat yourself kindly, attend to your physical and emotional health, engage your interests, develop your talents and skills, allow yourself pleasure and let yourself play. When you are balanced spiritually, mentally and physically, you are better able to give and receive love.

7. *Give Each Other Space to Grow.* If you've been ignored or abandoned in the past, you may have a tendency to be clingy. The thought of being apart might make you feel insecure. Remember, in mature love, individuality and autonomy must be honored. Time apart can be extremely valuable, as absence does make the heart grow fonder, and romance can be rekindled by the excitement of returning to each other's arms. Don't smother your love with possessiveness. Periods of separation will also make you more interesting to one another, by providing new stories to share.

Who Can Benefit from this Book

The Love Fitness Program has already proven valuable to many thousands of people. It can serve you well as a marriage manual. Clients report that mastering these emotional workouts provides the tools to create and sustain a vibrant, deeply rewarding love relationship.

For those readers who are considering marriage, congratulations! In general, married people are happier, healthier and wealthier than their single counterparts, according to sociological surveys. Marriage, however, is not an automatic ticket to live "happily ever after," but rather an opportunity to become a

4. One of the great benefits of this program is the prevention of serious problems. This book should therefore be of tremendous value to any couple considering marriage. It will assist you in exploring your relationship more deeply before making a lifetime commitment. If you are in a long-term love relationship already, the exercises will further enrich it.

Everyone who reads this book is likely to respond differently. Some exercises may be more directly applicable to you and your love relationship than others. In working your way through this book, practice the exercises you find most useful. If a particular emotional workout is inappropriate for your present needs, set it aside for now. Trust the wisdom within you.

Inner Peace: A Key to Relationship Harmony

You cannot have peace in your love relationship (or any relationship, for that matter) without cultivating it within yourself. Having a stable interior enables you to work out conflicts in your relationship with greater skill, love and caring. Of course, the peace I am referring to is not the listless placidity or the sedated repose that comes from alcohol or illicit drugs. It is not a sleepy peace, nor a dull lethargic peace, nor an "I can't be bothered" peace. Rather, it is a vibrant peace marked by a tranquil and responsive nervous system, steady but spirited emotions and a focused, fully attentive mind.

There is a wide spectrum of inner peace, ranging from ordinary relaxation to the illumined state of spiritual masters. The deeper you penetrate your inner core of peace, the more clearly you think and perceive, the more balanced you feel emotionally and the more your love relationship can thrive.

The following suggestions will help you create inner peace in better, richer person.

The modern marriage requires more than love if it is going to succeed. Life's complexities necessitate that you and your partner learn to understand the psychology of your "couple-dom," that is, the emotional dynamics of your evolving relationship. You can prevent unnecessary crises and catastrophes by learning Love Fitness skills now. Moreover, you will have the tools to create the marriage you really want.

The exercises in this book can help you improve not only your relationship with your partner, but also with children, parents and friends. The principles, strategies and techniques you will learn have universal benefits.

Most of the emotional workouts are intended to be practiced by couples. However, you do not currently have to be in a relationship to find value in the program. The exercises will help you attract and sustain a new, more deeply satisfying love relationship. Many of the emotional workouts can also be practiced with a close friend.

The Love Fitness Program is a breakthrough in four principal ways:

1. It provides a step-by-step path out of the fear, anger and hopelessness that arise when a love relationship is in trouble.
2. It develops specific emotional strengths and communication skills in those areas you need to become more competent. It helps you learn to deal with intense, uncomfortable feelings such as rage, anger and jealousy.
3. It provides specific exercises for practical results on a daily basis. There is nothing like tangible emotional success to increase confidence in yourself and your relationship. These workouts are designed to generate emotional breakthroughs that can soon blossom into great adventures of the heart.

the midst of everyday life. They will keep your body tranquil yet responsive, adaptive and energetic, while your mind is focused, steady and clear. Valuable under any circumstances, you'll find these recommendations especially helpful as you work through the exercises in this book:

1. *Practice the deep breath of peace.* In the midst of turmoil, peace is as close as your breath. When you are tense or upset, your breathing tends to be shallow and rapid, delivering less oxygen to your cells. When you are at peace, you breathe slowly and deeply. A vital component of your new repertoire, therefore, is learning to reverse the stress response by taking slow, deep breaths. Scientific research shows that people who practice breathing exercises daily cut their levels of stress and tension in half.

Get in the habit of breathing from your abdomen, not from the upper chest as most people do. Try breathing in through your nose, pushing your abdomen out as you inhale. This moves your diaphragm downward, allowing oxygen to enter the lower portion of your lungs. As the breath continues, on the inhale expand your chest, filling the rest of your lungs. When you exhale, draw in your abdomen. This makes the out breath slightly longer than usual, allowing stale air to leave your lungs.

Here is a simple yogic breathing exercise that can be practiced regularly to restore peace to your system. Sit comfortably with your back relaxed but straight. Loosen your clothing so you can easily expand your abdomen. Gently close your eyes. Using your right hand, close your right nostril with your thumb, and exhale through the left nostril to a slow count of six. Hold the exhale for a count of six. Inhale through the left nostril to a count of six. Close the left nostril with your ring finger and pinky and hold the inhale for a count of six. Now release your thumb and exhale through the right nostril to a count of six. Hold the exhale for a count of six, and then inhale through the same (right) nostril, for a count of six. Hold the inhale to a count of six. Exhale through the left nostril to a count of six. Continue to alternate nostrils, breathing in this sequence: exhale - hold - inhale - hold - switch nostrils, exhale - hold - inhale - hold - switch nostrils, for three minutes. Keep your attention focused on your breathing. With practice, this breathing exercise can steadily foster inner peace.

In addition, some people find it effective to repeat silently a word, mantra or sound to focus the mind as the breath goes in and out. For the inhale, words like *peace, one, Christ* or *God* are often used. For exhalation, consider using the sound *hu* (pronounced like the name Hugh). *Hu* is an ancient word meaning power, and is the root of several English words such as human, humor and huge.

2. *Fill your love life with music.* Scientific studies have documented that the right rhythms, melodies and lyrics can calm, heal and inspire. We don't need research to tell us that music can alleviate tension, release pent-up emotions and evoke peaceful feelings. Music can reduce the level of stress hormones, blood pressure, respiratory rate and contraction of the stomach and intestines. Truly, music can soothe the savage beast within.

The music does not have to be slow and soft to have a peaceful effect. Choose high-quality music that suits your needs at any particular moment. At times, something as soul-stirring as Beethoven's Ninth or a gospel choir might be just the thing to bring peace to your soul. At other times, pop songs that evoke special memories of happy times in your love relationship might do the trick. Whatever you choose, let it absorb you so completely that you become at one with the music.

3. *Laugh often.* Keep fun and laughter in your love life on a daily basis. Post cartoons on your refrigerator; listen to tapes of great comedians as you drive. Above all, learn to laugh at your

foibles. While your problem may be serious and your pain real, if you look hard enough, you can also find some absurdity in it to share with your partner.

There is a certain peace in not taking yourself too seriously. As G. K. Chesterton put it, "Angels can fly because they take themselves so lightly." Even if the road sometimes seems marked by blisters rather than bliss, it is wise to remember to lighten up.

4. *Pray regularly*. Set aside time for daily prayer. You may wish to create a sacred space in your home to pray. Direct your prayers to the God, Higher Power or Presence of your understanding. Some feel most comfortable reciting a traditional prayer from a sacred text or religious tradition they follow. Others prefer to speak spontaneously in their own words. You may find a prayer of your own already inscribed in your heart, or you may wish to let the rhythm of your soul make it up as you go along. Feeling that you and your partner are loved by God is a powerful bond to strengthen daily.

I encourage you to approach the work ahead as a sacred quest. Creating peace and passion in your love relationship is seldom a straightforward, linear journey with a neat beginning, middle and end. It meanders, it winds, it moves in fits and starts, with bursts of speedy progress mixed with apparent setbacks and roadblocks. It can be a joyful, exhilarating ride, but at other times it can be challenging. Along the way you may have to give up your resentments, your anger, your fears, your arrogance, your grandiosity and feeling victimized. You may have to forgive yourself for not being "perfect" and also learn to accept your love partner as he or she is. Is it worth it? Your peace of mind and the quality of your love life is at stake. There is perhaps no greater challenge than the adventure of the heart's quest to love and be loved.

Chapter 2

Three Magic Words for a Happy Relationship

EARLY ON IN MOST RELATIONSHIPS, couples tend to hang on each other's every word. The excitement of discovery of another person's feelings, opinions and needs is so enthralling that new partners can't pay enough attention to one another. Over time, that enthusiasm for listening wears off. Couples tend to think they know one another and lose interest in probing deeper. It becomes easy to pretend to be listening while reading the paper, watching TV or driving the car. In reality, one or the other may be tuned out. Couples who come for counseling have almost always developed an inability to listen to one another. Have you ever thought about or complained to your partner in any of the following ways?

- "I'm not going to tell you how I feel because when and if I try to, you don't hear me. You become defensive and angry and you jump in with your views and opinions. Whenever we actually talk about anything important, I feel like I have to compete to get a word in. It's impossible for me to let you know how I feel, because you are so defensive."

- "When you go out of control in an argument, you make it very clear that I'm not allowed to express my true feelings. You'll never change, so why should I even bother being open with you?"
- "You do a very good job of pointing out my faults. You belittle me in front of other people. Then you joke about it, as if you think it's funny. I end up apologizing for my shortcomings, just to appease you."
- "I can't ever tell you how I feel about something, without you threatening me or tuning out. You won't let me know what you're really feeling, unless you get mad."
- "So often, I agree with you just to shut you up and keep the peace. I don't think you'll ever understand how I feel. I'm going to hold back my affection, too. I'll pour my love into other things, like the children and my work, but not you."
- "I feel like I always have to be on my toes, because anything I say might throw you into a tizzy. I allow you to intimidate me, which causes me to feel even more hurt and angry. My stinging comments are like poison darts because I'm enraged with you. The situation feels hopeless, and I feel powerless."

You may resent not being heard by your partner, yet you may fail to appreciate that he or she also needs to feel validated. When you feel misunderstood, you tend to blame each other. You each become so involved in defending yourselves, that you fail to hear each other needs.

The "Tell Me More" Exercise

At my seminars, some participants joke that the three magic words are "Yes, I will" (do whatever you say). While cooperation is, of course, essential, compliance eventually breeds resentment. Most think "I love you" are the three magic words. Regularly affirming your love is important and, indeed, the bedrock of your relationship. However, to grow your relationship, you also need a magical incantation to dissolve conflict, speak from the depths of your heart and validate the most intimate feelings and essence of one another.

The three magic words are "Tell me more." The phrase "tell me more" is a seemingly simple yet powerful tool that will help couples achieve a breakthrough in the quality and emotional depth of their communication.

When you say, "Tell me more," you give your partner your undivided attention and respect. It shows you care and that what is being said is important to you. How often have you wished your partner would say those three words? How often have you instead found yourself frustrated, with feelings you really needed to share? How often have you been afraid to express yourself because you were afraid of your partner's reaction? How often have you thought, "Why bother?" because your partner was not receptive?

By using the phrase "Tell me more," you will enhance your ability to listen as well as upgrade the quality of attention you give your partner. Sometimes it is extremely difficult to listen to your partner. This is particularly true when your partner needs to express feelings of frustration, anger or criticism. The natural response to such an emotional onslaught is to become defensive. Although they are natural, responses such as "Yes, but . . ." or "Wait, listen to me for a moment. . ." prevent you from acknowledging, absorbing and learning from what your partner has to say.

Few emotional tasks are more difficult than hearing and accepting a partner's anger, hurt and criticism without becoming defensive. The inability to communicate openly about difficult emotional issues is a serious problem in most relationships.

Many couples benefit from a structured exercise to assist them in dealing with charged emotions and especially upsetting issues. I call this workout the "Tell Me More" exercise. The basic steps are as follows:

1. Find a room in which you both feel safe and relaxed. This room should be pleasant and comfortable. Adding flowers, candles and incense can be a nice touch. Turn off your phones and put a "Do Not Disturb" sign on the door to ensure privacy.

2. Arrange two chairs so you and your partner are facing each other. Sit close enough to feel in contact, but not so close that you violate each other's comfort zone. A conversational distance is best.

3. The suggestion to try the "Tell Me More" exercise is usually made by the person who needs to have some feelings resolved. If you notice that your partner is upset, however, you need not wait for him or her to suggest the exercise. Rather, you can initiate this process as a way of clearing the air and reestablishing emotional contact.

4. The listener restricts his or her statements to one phrase, "Tell me more." It is critical that this phrase not be said casually or mechanically. There is a natural rhythm to conversation and particularly to self-revelation. If one of you is courageous enough to express blocked feelings, the other must use the phrase "Tell me more" as a safe and sincere expression of interest.

5. When one partner has thoroughly expressed his or her feelings, switch roles. The other now has the same opportunity to express any feelings in response to the phrase "Tell me more." The exercise is not over until both partners feel better. Always finish with a warm hug and each say, "I love you."

Here is an example of the "Tell Me More" process. It should give you a better understanding of how this exercise works in practice.

Jessica: I am so angry with you. We haven't gone out in such a long time. We've been so busy, and on our one night out . . . what do you do? The whole evening, you didn't pay any attention to me; you kept staring at and talking to that brunette in the red dress. I felt embarrassed and humiliated. She was an attractive woman, but that was ridiculous!

Dave: Tell me more.

Jessica: I feel that I can't go out without worrying about who you will flirt with. As it is, we have so little social time together that when we're together, I want to feel that you enjoy being with me. I don't mean you should talk to me the entire time, but I want to feel that you've given me some quality attention. I want to feel like you really want to be with me. I'm afraid sometimes . . . that you're bored with me. After all these years of being together, I'm starting to think you don't want me. I'm afraid you're ready to move on, that you want to be with somebody else.

Dave [quietly]: Tell me more.

Jessica: I want to trust you. I don't want to think that your looking at other women might be a reflection on our relationship. I want to be able to trust you.

Dave: Tell me more.

Jessica: I love you and I love being with you. I want us to have something of the romance that we had in the beginning of our relationship. It feels good to be able to tell you this.

Dave: Tell me more.

Jessica: I love you. I feel better that I got this off my chest.

Dave: I love you, too. [Dave and Jessica get up and embrace . . . long pause.]

Dave: I respect what you've said, and I would like to get some of my feelings and perceptions out, too. Okay?

Jessica: Of course. Let's sit down.

Dave: I'm surprised. I just can't believe you. We go to a party, I have a conversation with a woman who happens to be attractive and suddenly I'm ignoring you. I mean, I don't think that marriage is supposed to be a ball and chain, where I have to be careful with whom I have a conversation. If I meet someone at a party, I can only say, 'Hi, how are you? Are you over eighty years old or under eight? Well, good, but then I can only talk to you for five minutes, okay? Then I've got to go back to my wife.' I feel like I don't have any freedom. Same as my father had in his relationship. There's no space. No freedom at all. And it just pisses me off! I wasn't doing anything so terrible last night, but when you're staring at me all the time, it doesn't make me want to come over to you. It's more like, 'Hey, forget this! Let me have some quality attention over here!' You know? I don't need those dagger-eyes of yours. I feel controlled and manipulated by your jealousy.

Jessica: Tell me more.

Dave: It makes me sad. I want to be married to you, I love you, but I also need some space to feel free. I need to feel that I'm still my own person, like I can have a conversation with someone even if they are attractive. I need to feel like that's okay.

Jessica: Tell me more.

Dave: You know I was single for a long time. You just don't suddenly change the habits of a lifetime. *[Dave laughs at himself and elicits a smile from Jessica.]*

Jessica: Tell me more, Dave.

Dave: It feels good to be able to get out these feelings I've been holding in. I've been feeling trapped, as if I'm on a leash. The angrier I feel, the more I want to get away from you. The truth is, I feel so free right now, being able to share these feelings with you. I've never been able to do this with anyone else. It feels really good *[pause and deep breath]*. It puts me in touch with just how much I love you. And you're right! I haven't been giving you enough quality attention. I'm going to make more time for you and me. We don't have to let our romance dwindle. We can rekindle it, when we choose to.

This "Tell Me More" workout was an emotional breakthrough for Dave and Jessica. For the first time, they felt safe enough with each other to be totally vulnerable. They saw how they were keeping each other from the innermost regions of their hearts because of their own fears and anger. They also saw they could release their pent-up feelings through heart-to-heart communication. The "Tell Me More" exercise is the cornerstone of the Love Fitness Program. Regular practice of this exercise helps to eliminate the suppressed anger that blocks peace and intimacy. It will open you up to one another as never before.

Do's and Don'ts of the "Tell Me More" Exercise

I usually recommend "Tell Me More" as the first exercise for creating peace and passion in your love relationship. My experience indicates that when partners express their feelings to one another fully and completely, the result is almost always positive. It is critical in this process, however, that you listen to your partner's feelings fully, no matter how much hurt, anger or resentment may be expressed. The point of the exercise is to release pent-up emotions in an atmosphere of safety and trust. Be patient; let the feelings unfold. *Underneath anger is hurt, and underneath hurt is love.* Once the underlying love surfaces, it naturally grows, healing the painful feelings and providing a renewed emotional base for correcting problems in the relationship.

Here are additional instructions for the "Tell Me More" exercise:

1. *Make "I" rather than "You" statements.* The word "I" is allowed; "you," which can often be perceived as an accusation, is not. Statements that begin with "you" often make the listener feel under attack and defensive. An "I" statement is much more likely to be received with receptive ears. Example: "You're so rigid and inflexible," would instead be stated, "I experienced you as rigid and inflexible in that circumstance."

2. *Don't interrupt.* The key to the "Tell Me More" exercise is never to interrupt your partner and only to respond with one simple phrase, "Tell me more." When faced with your partner's expression of anger or criticism, you may feel tempted to interrupt, to deny that his or her views make any sense, to make explanations or excuses, or to make your partner feel guilty, stupid or awkward. In order for the "Tell Me More" exercise to work, you must guard against becoming reactive and defensive. The correct response is to pause, breathe deeply, relax yourself, and repeat, "Tell me more."

3. *Don't start the exercise if you're excessively tired or preoccupied.* To do this workout effectively, you must be reasonably well rested. It takes energy, and can be emotionally intense and demanding on you and your partner. You can't expect an emotional workout to go well if you start it off feeling exhausted. Similarly, if either of you is preoccupied with problems about work, money or children, it is better to postpone the exercise. Judgment is required here. Although preoccupation with outside pressures shouldn't become an excuse to avoid intimate

communication, be sensitive to this issue. The key is to use this exercise as a tool for emotional release and bonding.

4. *Accept your partner's feelings and point of view without judgment.* Be attentive and receptive, and not judgmental. Your partner may say things to which you want to make a rebuttal. You are giving your partner the gifts of safety, freedom and unconditional love when you cultivate receptive listening.

5. *Don't be impatient.* This exercise cannot be hurried because no one can rush the expression of feelings. Sitting on the edge of your seat blurting, "Tell me more...tell me more," won't create the safety and trust necessary to share difficult feelings. When your mind is jumping to respond, even with the phrase "tell me more," you're not listening well and your partner will feel it. Relax and put yourself into as receptive a mode as possible.

6. *Don't be contemptuous or arrogant.* It is possible to fake participation in the "Tell Me More" exercise by giving the false impression that you are listening when in fact your mind is tuned-out. This arrogance allows you to defend yourself internally from your partner's hurt, anger or frustration by silently demeaning his or her words. Such contempt stands in the way of genuine listening. Be simple, humble and open to learning.

7. *Don't jump to conclusions.* Listen to your partner's words and the feelings that underlie those words. Don't assume that you know the outcome when your partner expresses a recurring set of feelings. Rather than jump to conclusions, maintain an attitude of discovery. Show respect for your partner's emotional life and intelligence by listening without preconception.

8. *Sit in an open-body position.* Eighty percent of communication is non-verbal. A rolling of the eyes can

communicate more than the actual words said. It is best to sit in an open body position with your arms and legs uncrossed, directly facing one another. This posture signals you are being open and sensitive to your partner.

9. *Give full and undivided attention.* In this world of multi-tasking, it is so easy to be distracted or let our attention wander. Through facial expression, eye contact and body language let your partner know that what they are saying is important to you. Giving your partner your full attention demonstrates that you honor and respect who they are.

10. *Be empathic.* The goal of this exercise is to let your partner know that you acknowledge and accept what they feel. This does not mean you have to agree. The more empathetic and understanding you can be, the more your partner will feel safe and loved. Instead of trying to convince your partner to feel differently, listen patiently and be compassionate.

11. *Take a time-out if needed.* Either partner can ask for a fifteen- to twenty-minute time-out. Even if you prefer to continue communicating what you feel upset about, allow your partner that quiet time to regroup and settle down. It is important to honor that we each have a different tolerance for emotionally charged communication. As Ralph Waldo Emerson said, "We boil at different degrees."

Just as there are do's and don'ts as a listener in the "Tell Me More" exercise, there are precepts to follow as a speaker:

1. *Don't be afraid to say what you feel.* The purpose of this exercise is to communicate your feelings as thoroughly and deeply as possible. Only by expressing your feelings in depth can you achieve true resolution, avoid storing resentment and discover grounds for better communication.

2. *Don't make your partner bad or wrong.* There is a fine line

between communicating hurt feelings and destructively dumping, berating or shaming. You are allowed to get angry and express frustration and pain. However, it is not valuable to indulge in demeaning invectives such as, "You're a liar," "You never do anything right," or "You're crazy." Such vitriolic is meant to put down, punish or manipulate, and the effects are negative and destructive.

3. *Don't rush yourself.* Feelings unfold gradually. You may begin with feelings of frustration which, when acknowledged, give rise to deeper feelings of hurt, anger or resentment. If you give full expression to those feelings, it is likely that beneath the anger, fear and pain are deeper feelings of love, care and commitment. Only by following the "Tell Me More" exercise to its conclusion can loving feelings fully reemerge.

4. *Focus on one issue.* Be specific about exactly what behavior or incident upset you. There may be many conflicts to address, but the exercise works best if you select one issue at a time and pursue it to resolution. Other issues can wait until another time.

5. *Acknowledge your vulnerabilities and weaknesses.* Simple, humble communication is necessary. It is important that you share your weaknesses and acknowledge your "dark side." Some examples are, "I can be selfish and controlling," or "I feel jealousy and rage" and "I hate myself for lying."

6. *Be willing to forgive.* Trying to forgive before you share pent-up hurt and resentment can lead to incomplete healing. Express your anger fully, but then try to look past the acts themselves and see the pain, fear and emotional wounds behind them—not to find excuses, but to comprehend and understand. Healing a major betrayal, however, may require a therapist or counselor to act as a facilitator.

Two Powerful Emotional Gifts

So there you have the "Tell Me More" exercise. It is perhaps the single most important emotional workout for keeping a relationship fit and vital. This is not an overstatement, because this exercise will allow you to reap two powerful emotional gifts:

1. You will learn how to accept your partner's hurt, anger and criticism without becoming defensive. As a result, you and your partner will develop greater emotional strength and freedom to communicate.
2. You will receive quality feedback about your opinions, perceptions and behaviors. Constructive feedback allows you and your relationship to grow.

When you can accept your partner's hurt, anger and criticism without becoming defensive, you:

• Demonstrate unconditional love, care and respect for your partner.
• Help your partner stop hurting by allowing difficult feelings to be expressed, without interruption or comment.
• Strengthen the care and trust between you by listening to painful feelings with compassion and understanding.

Primary Principles for Developing Love Fitness

Love Fitness workouts are similar to physical fitness exercises in another important respect. If you pace yourself, they can be enjoyable and healthful. If you try to accomplish too much too soon, they can be laborious or even injurious. The following guidelines will help you use the program to your best advantage:

- *Take the initiative.* It is very easy to let yourself feel defeated when you are unhappy with your relationship. Until you practice a few Love Fitness workouts, you won't be able to see how much power you really have. No doubt you can think of many reasons why you, your partner or the relationship can't change, and you could spend hours in therapy talking about all those reasons.

  The real challenge is to first break just one old negative emotional habit. Don't try for all at once. Start simply by selecting an emotional workout that particularly appeals to you. Making your partner responsible for its success won't help, although you have the right to ask for his or her participation. Change always begins with you. Don't focus on changing your partner, even "for his or her own good."

- *Re-evaluate your "comfort zone."* Many people get quite comfortable with feeling uncomfortable! Starting to feel more genuinely intimate and loving may initially leave you feeling uneasy, fearful or even strange. One of the first things you may experience when you practice a Love Fitness workout is "This isn't me–it doesn't feel natural." This initial response is to be expected because emotional workouts develop new relationship habits and self-perceptions. Think for a moment how you felt when you first learned to ride a bicycle, ski or play tennis. You probably felt a little awkward, and perhaps somewhat foolish. You may even have felt you'd never learn to develop the grace and coordination required. However, with practice, hundreds of repetitions later, the new habit became automatic and felt completely natural.

  When you practice an exercise intended to expand your behavioral repertoire or change an emotional response, you should definitely expect to feel some initial awkwardness. As you practice the exercise, you will develop a new and valued way of relating to yourself and others. Ways of responding that may initially seem mechanical will soon start to feel graceful. Give yourself the time and permission to overcome any initial feelings of discomfort. Your "comfort zone" will stretch to include a completely new experience of the heart.

- *Stretch, don't strain.* In this program, significant changes are going to occur on very intimate levels of feeling for yourself and your partner. Delicate personal energies are involved. You won't achieve the desired growth if you push yourself into changing. You can't benefit by setting up absolute demands and then becoming angry with yourself if you don't meet them. If an exercise doesn't seem to help you achieve a result on a particular day, set it aside and try again tomorrow. Be disciplined with yourself, but also gentle and patient.

    Growth is a natural process that does not need to be forced. An acorn doesn't strain to become an oak tree; neither must you strain to grow. In a physical fitness program, you would be cautioned against overdoing it, which can lead to discomfort, injury and loss of motivation. The same principle applies to the Love Fitness Program.

- *Nobody is perfect.* There are times in every relationship when one or both people "blow it." It is important to understand at such moments that Love Fitness is not some idealized concept. Don't become disillusioned or cynical if you make an "emotional mistake." Rather, acknowledge your error and find a way to reestablish heart-to-heart communication as quickly as possible. The best way to begin is with a simple, direct and heartfelt apology. By apologizing and asking for forgiveness, you can heal the emotional breach and learn from your mistakes.

- *Repetition is the key to mastery.* Developing Love Fitness is a learning process. I explain to clients and seminar participants that to make lasting changes, regular workouts are needed. No one is a one-trial learner!

As adults, we tend to feel foolish and awkward when learning something new. Watching my then one-year-old daughter, Shazara, take her first steps, I learned a powerful lesson: It's not how many times you fall, but how many times you get back up. Everyone learned to walk by first stumbling and falling many times. Developing Love Fitness is no different; accept that failure and vulnerability are an essential part of mastering heart-to-heart communication skills.

All psychological growth involves insight and behavior change. You must put the insights and techniques into practice. In learning a musical instrument or athletic skill, repetition is the key to success. It is the same with Love Fitness; exercises must be practiced regularly if you are to achieve the desired results.

- *Difficulties and challenges will always arise.* There is no permanent victory in life; problems and challenges will always arise. Growth is never in a straight upward line. With its twists and turns, it is more often a swerving path. You may reach a new plateau of understanding with your partner only to encounter a crisis that sets you back. There is a common tendency to revert to old emotional habits under stress, particularly in love relationships. Don't despair if that happens. Use "back-sliding" as a new opportunity to solidify and increase your progress. Use problems as an opportunity for further growth.

- Make Love Fitness an adventure. This program is not meant to establish a rigid, monolithic standard. Rather, it is intended to be enjoyable and exciting, an adventure in self-development and mutual discovery. Once you achieve one or two specific goals, you may experience a shift in the perception of your relationship from one of frustration and problems to one of abundance and joy. Where you once felt constricted, you will start to see opportunities for adventure and love.

Making the Love Fitness Program Your Own

It is important to understand the reason for structured exercises. Love Fitness workouts encourage the communication of powerful, intense feelings. Though guidelines may seem mechanical, they provide structure, safety and a framework for sharing challenging emotions. Structured exercises allow for truly spontaneous, heartfelt expression of feelings. Once you have mastered the basic form, the instructions are not intended to be forever rigid and monolithic. I expect you will adapt the words in the exercises to your own way of speaking. However, I also expect that in adapting the exercises you will be careful to observe the essential principles and rules.

Regarding getting started, a simple and direct approach is best in inviting a partner to join you. You might suggest your partner read this book, or even just part of it. You could offer the opportunity of taking a few minutes to try one of the workouts as an experiment. Make the suggestion in an open, non-demanding way. Emphasize that the exercise can be a learning experience and an opportunity to draw both of you closer. It is valuable to discuss an exercise before you try it. Listen to your partner's views and concerns about participating. Be respectful, even if he or she appears cynical. You are not attempting to "fix" your partner or prove that what he or she is doing is wrong.

Gradually the "Tell Me More" exercise becomes a spontaneous way of responding to your partner when you notice his or her tension, hurt or anger. You won't have to sit down to go through the whole formal process. You can use "Tell Me More" in the kitchen, the car, at the beach–wherever it might be appropriate at the time. This key Love Fitness skill can become deeply rewarding in every aspect of your life.

Chapter 3

Heart Talks
For Greater Intimacy

CONNECTING HEART-TO-HEART is the great joy and purpose of a love relationship. Intimacy can be thought of as "into-me-see." Can you and your partner freely reveal to each other who you really are and what you really want with all your strengths and weaknesses, hopes and fears, successes and failure?

For some couples, the answer at best is a qualified yes, but for many it is "no." Most people are afraid to let others, even a partner, know what they really feel about important personal issues. For example, sexual anxiety remains widespread, but most couples rarely talk about it enough to allay their fears. Although frustration in achieving personal goals may be discussed, few couples take the time to explore their deepest hopes. Lack of self-confidence, hidden resentments, painful memories and secret desires are universal, but few couples know how to help each other accept and resolve these powerful inner feelings.

Most couples spend less than thirty minutes per week sharing their most intimate feelings; no wonder relationships go stale. Rather than explore their feelings, many couples assume they know how each other feels, when in reality, they are each afraid to ask! For love to remain exciting and vibrant, intense and deeply honest communication of feelings is vital. This chapter is about accepting that challenge and creating an adventure of mutual discovery.

To begin, an assessment of fears that stand in the way of heart-to-heart communication is helpful. For some people, a fear of rejection is a primary inhibition. Almost everyone harbors some anxiety that if a partner really knew everything, rejection might result. Other people fear their own anger. They resist exposing their deepest feelings because they are afraid of confrontation or having an argument. Still others fear an encounter with their own self-image. They fear that letting a partner know them will be humiliating, or lead them to feel inferior. Those who desperately sought love and found it may discover a new worry–the fear of losing that love, and once again being left to face life alone. The persistence of such fears makes creating and sustaining a great love relationship difficult, if not impossible.

The following comments, from participants in my seminars, illustrate common fears in love relationships:

"Our relationship has gone flat; I feel like you've become bored with me."

"If my partner knew the real me, she would leave."

"I get to a certain point in a relationship where I feel blocked and I want to flee."

"After we have sex, I feel lonely and disconnected."

"I'm afraid to risk my heart again; I don't want to get hurt."

"I don't feel loved or appreciated; we share the same house, the same bed, yet much of the time I feel like we're strangers."

Withholding such feelings creates a burden on you and your relationship by undermining self-confidence and blocking the flow of love. When two people hide their deepest feelings, the relationship is doomed to boredom and chronic frustration. Instead of making their needs clear, couples begin to manipulate, intimidate and blame each other. Alienation, affairs and divorce often follow.

Overcoming Fears of Self-Disclosure

How do you overcome the fears of self-disclosure that block heart-to-heart communication with your partner? I have developed a series of Love Fitness workouts called Heart Talks. Heart Talks establish an environment of care, safety and trust, allowing you and your partner to enjoy greater self-disclosure and a deeper love connection. Those who learn Heart Talks report that these exercises are challenging, exciting and often life-transforming.

Heart Talks involve much more than saccharine sentimentality. They are designed to help you discover the courage to be vulnerable, to divulge insecurities, to work through conflict and to share your dreams and hopes. Heart Talks instill the safety and trust necessary to do the psychological housecleaning that every intimate relationship requires.

Even if your partner is uncooperative at first, the more self-disclosing you are, the more open and honest your partner is likely to be. Heart Talks are an opportunity to look in the mirror of relationship. You come to your partner not only as a separate being, but also as a mirror of each other's moods and attitudes. If you have critical thoughts about her, she is more likely to be critical of you. If you think loving thoughts about him, he is more likely to be loving to you.

Heart Talks can serve to benefit you and your love relationship in the following ways:

1. *Creating emotional safety.* You and your partner can create safety and trust to talk about whatever might be disturbing you.

2. *Releasing tension.* Every love relationship will encounter rough points and accumulate frustration; Heart Talks are a way of clearing the air.

3. *Nurturing and connecting.* Heart-to-heart communication nurtures you and your partner in a way that no amount of physical sex alone can provide. It is a means to experience greater intimacy and connectedness on every level of your being.

4. *Learning more about yourself.* Some people shy away from intimacy because they fear going deeper into themselves. Heart Talks allow you to discover more about yourself and then share what you learn with your partner.

5. *Feeling affirmed, understood and accepted.* No matter how autonomous and independent you may be, it is important to feel acknowledged and understood by your partner. Heart Talks help you and your partner make sure that each of you gets the affirmation and acceptance you need.

6. *Having fun.* Heart Talks are more than serious emotional conversations; they're also a means to add spice, delight and humor.

7. *Rediscovering your partner.* In the business of everyday life, it is easy to take your partner for granted and assume you know what he or she thinks. Heart Talks are a means

of discovering recent changes in your partner's feelings, ideas and goals.

8. *Energizing a love relationship.* Heart Talks allow you and your partner to experience new heights of passion by strengthening the bonds of intimacy. You will discover ways of enjoying one another that you might not have even thought possible.

9. *Healing yourself.* Heart Talks provide an opportunity to make peace with your "dark side." To love deeply, each of us must accept any disowned feelings of hostility, fear and rage that lie within. Heart Talks allow for understanding the seemingly contradictory forces of love and hate. When love partners learn to embrace each other's dark sides, they also become more compassionate with themselves.

10. *Forgiving.* To forgive fully requires that you acknowledge your hurt and appropriately give voice to any pent-up resentment. Heart Talks give you an opportunity to express all your feelings so you can truly forgive.

Heart Talks can revitalize a long-term relationship as well as deepen the experience of those newly in love. For the reader who is not currently in a love relationship, these exercises will be valuable to practice with a close friend. You will acquire tools and skills for being more open, as well as helping your partner to become more open, which is the surest way to ensure a peaceful, passionate love relationship.

Pent-up emotions produce wear and tear on the nervous system and gradually erode heath. Chronic stress is a major cause of many failed marriages. Many couples find they can dramatically reduce tension as a result of self-disclosure. What you feel you can heal; what you share you can repair.

Heart Talks can help heavy pressures become lighter. With some exercises, sharing dissolves into laughter and tears of joy. They can help you stop taking yourself so seriously and discover that we as humans have the same fears, needs and hopes.

Heart Blocks

If intimacy is so wonderful and yields such benefits, why is the fear of self-disclosure so widespread? The primary reason, as I have said, is that most people were exposed to negative emotional habits in early childhood. They saw their parents engage in destructive conflict, emotional withdrawal or both. Since their parents weren't models for intimate conversation, they never learned to communicate safely and appropriately.

Another reason is that while new relationships are propelled by the excitement of romance, many couples get so caught up in their everyday lives–career, finances, children–that they stop putting energy into their relationship without realizing it. They allow themselves to get "emotionally flabby" and don't work as hard to maintain intimacy.

Before you begin your workouts with Heart Talks, gaining insight into your "heart blocks" is helpful. Read the following statements and mark each one true or false as it applies to you:

1. There are some things I'm just too embarrassed or ashamed to admit.
2. If I am open and vulnerable, my partner will perceive me as weak and lose respect for me.
3. If I share my true feelings, my partner will get angry or withdraw.
4. If I am completely open, it will be used against me.
5. As soon as a relationship gets serious, I worry it will end.
6. I want to be more intimate, but I just can't find the right person.
7. I worry that my partner will grow bored with me; familiarity breeds contempt.
8. As I become more emotionally involved, I lose touch with

reality; work and other relationships suffer.

9. When it comes to intimacy, I feel that I give too much and get too little in return.

10. After my previous love relationship, I doubt that I can be totally open and intimate with someone again.

11. I'm afraid of being stuck in an unhappy marriage like the one my parents had.

12-20. I don't like to admit it, but sometimes when my partner wants to be close and reaches out to me:

- I seem to accept the feelings outwardly, but without letting them really touch me.
- I go into a monologue and become defensive.
- I behave in an arrogant, "above-it-all" fashion.
- I become analytical and intellectualize to stay away from my deeper feelings.
- I get irritated or start a fight.
- I pretend to be confused, saying I don't really understand what's being said or asked for.
- I make jokes to avoid intimate conversation.
- I change the subject or act as if the discussion isn't really important when compared to responsibilities and "real" business to be attended to.
- I suspect that my partner has hidden motives–wanting sex, permission to buy something, etc.

If you marked three or fewer of the statements as True, you open your heart freely and aren't afraid to be vulnerable.

If you marked four to eight of them as True, you open your heart halfway, depending on circumstances or the issues at hand.

If you marked nine to fourteen statements as True, you open your heart just a crack, to peek outside, to risk taking a further step.

If fifteen or more were marked as True, you keep the door to your heart locked and doubled-bolted.

Your score on this quiz is helpful in several ways. First, if you answered nine or more True, you can expect that exercising with Heart Talks will feel awkward at first. Remember, that is okay. Learning new emotional skills will stretch your comfort zone. Second, the Heart Talk exercises described in this chapter begin with relatively easy explorations, and lead to eventually sharing secrets, which is much more challenging. The higher your score, the more time you should spend with the easier exercises before going on to more challenging ones. Third, take another look at your answers, paying attention to those marked as True. You can gain valuable insight into how you might ward off intimacy (for example, by withdrawing, changing the subject or becoming intellectual). Be alert to dropping these habitual defenses during Heart Talk exercises.

Heart Talk Agreements

The rules for Heart Talk exercises are simple but very necessary. Strict adherence to these agreements ensures emotional safety and correct practice.

The first rule is the same as for the "Tell Me More" exercise–never interrupt. This is crucial for Heart Talks, since you take turns answering a question or completing a statement.

For many people, the habit of interrupting is so ingrained that it can occur despite their best intentions. To avoid the ensuing irritation and misunderstanding, I sometimes suggest utilizing a tool as a reminder not to interrupt: passing a small heart-shaped pillow back and forth. Whoever holds this Heart Talk pillow speaks without interruption. The other partner's response is confined to saying "tell me more." The Heart Talk pillow is a strong reminder not to interrupt. It should only be used for Heart Talks, as it will become very special to both of you, a symbol of your love, commitment and growth.

It is critical that each partner not be on any mind-altering substance, including alcohol. Sometimes people think they are more open or more self-disclosing when they have had "a couple of drinks." It is better to deal with your fears of being open and self-disclosing, than to alter your state with illicit drugs and alcohol.

Create a warm environment for your Heart Talks. Turn off the phones, and take precautions against outside interruption. In addition, until you learn to be "in close," it is important to set up a "proper distance." Use comfortable chairs placed three to three-and-a-half feet apart, allowing for eye contact and enough "space" to be able to deal with any difficult feelings that may emerge. As you grow more comfortable, you can move closer together. Some people like to sit cross-legged on the floor or bed, holding hands while maintaining eye contact. Do what feels best, but always face each other with an open body position.

Set a time limit at first–at least thirty minutes, but not more than one hour per sitting. This will preempt the tendency to "feel like quitting" when resistances come up. Just as with a physical fitness program, consistency is necessary. To get started, I suggest either three half-hour sessions or one full-hour session each week, to create greater intimacy with your partner.

Keep in mind that partners are not alike in their tolerance of, or desire for, intimacy. While almost everyone could use more intimacy, people have differences in pace, style and comfort that must be respected. Don't make your love partner wrong for being more hesitant or less gung ho than you are. In any case, both of you must honor your Heart Talk agreements, to create an atmosphere of mutual respect, safety and trust.

Rules are essential to feeling safe and secure when you have a Heart Talk. Each time you have a Heart Talk, both of you should review and agree to the following:

1. I promise not to withdraw emotionally, or to leave physically; I will not reject you for anything you share.
2. I will make it safe for you to express your most intimate feelings; I will stay open and receptive to you.
3. Nothing you say will be used against you, or to provoke an argument later.
4. I will be responsible for my emotions, and I will not blame you for how I feel. If I do blame or complain, I will take immediate responsibility for doing so and stop.
5. I will share the truth from my heart as caringly, honestly and respectfully as I can.
6. I will love you unconditionally and use any block or conflict that may arise to learn more and grow.
7. I will not try to manipulate, defend or control what you communicate.
8. I commit to dealing with and working through any barriers that may come up in our Heart Talks, until there is resolution and we once again feel loving toward each other.
9. I agree that we can disagree, and that we may not see eye-to-eye about all issues. We may have very different feelings and points of view, and that's okay.
10. I agree to finish each Heart Talk session with at least one big hug (remember, five hugs a day keeps the marriage counselor away) and a sincere "I love you."

These agreements are so important that I suggest you photocopy them, or keep the book open to this page during your Heart Talks. Take turns reading aloud these agreements before you begin your Heart Talks.

Levels of Intimacy

The Heart Talk diagram below depicts four levels of intimacy and personal privacy. Level S represents the subject of Secrets; Level A is for Ambivalences; Level F is for Feelings; and Level E is for Explorations.

These levels of intimacy form the acronym S.A.F.E., a reminder of the key element for Heart Talks. An emotional environment of total trust and safety allows you to be completely vulnerable. This can gradually afford personal liberation from fear, and therefore a higher quality of love. Your heart becomes more transparent, encircled by your soul and spirit.

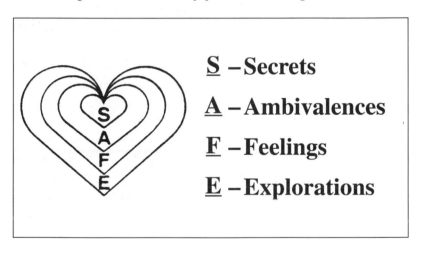

S – **Secrets**

A – **Ambivalences**

F – **Feelings**

E – **Explorations**

Level E (Explorations) covers emotionally neutral information. In this zone, communication consists primarily of explorations of points of view, beliefs and attitudes on topics such as "What I like best/least about my work is . . ." and "My views on homeland security and national defense are . . ."

At level F (Feelings), you begin to communicate your feelings and desires, for example, "I feel frustrated . . ." "I am optimistic about . . ." "I hope . . ." "I look forward to..."

At level A (Ambivalences), you share conflicted feelings about yourself, your love relationship and family life. Sometimes the block to intimacy is that we have trouble expressing our mixed emotions: "I'm confused about . . ." "Sometimes I wonder if we'll make it . . ."

Level S (Secrets) is the innermost level of intimacy. This level represents the territory of hidden feelings and buried fears such as "I feel ashamed of . . ." "Ever since I can remember, I've been afraid of . . ." Most people keep the content of level S (Secrets), as well as level A (Ambivalences), a wholly private concern. They share these thoughts, feelings and wishes with no one, thereby severing a crucial link to deeper intimacy. If you are somewhat open, you can share from these innermost levels of the heart with perhaps one or two special people whom you trust completely.

Communicating Heart-to-Heart

For a Heart Talk session, take turns completing sentences or answering questions from an agreed-upon level. Remember to review your Heart Talk rules before commencing each workout. To get comfortable with Heart Talks, it is good to begin where it might be the easiest, Explorations, then move onto Feelings, then Ambivalences, then finally Secrets.

Heart Talks–Level E: Explorations
1. Three people in history I would most like to have as dinner guests are . . .
2. The personal and professional business goals I want to accomplish this year are . . . in the next five years are. . .
3. A one-month, all-expenses-paid trip I would like to take anywhere in the world is. . .
4. The three people who have most influenced my values

and thinking are . . .

5. My feelings about gay and lesbian marriage are . . .
6. What I would do to end world hunger is . . .
7. My views on abortion are . . .
8. How I feel about divorce is . . .
9. The way to raise children is . . .
10. My feelings about being/becoming a parent are . . .
11. I would like to spend more of our time . . .
12. What I like best/least about my work and career is...
13. If I could have three magic wishes, they would be...
14. My religious beliefs are . . .
15. God, in my view, is . . .
16. My views on combating terrorism versus protecting civil liberties are...
17. What I feel to be crucial to foster world peace is . . .
18. The meaning of life is...

Here are some fun yet revealing questions to consider:

19. If your partner were to be an item of food, what would he or she be? Why? Describe why you chose this particular food to represent your partner.
20. If your partner were to be an animal, what animal would he or she be? Again, describe why

Heart Talks–Level F: Feelings

1. What I am upset about is...
2. I am angry and resentful that...
3. I feel hurt that...
4. I feel most loved when...
5. What concerns or worries me most is. . .
6. An important change I would like to see in you is . . .
7. If I could change one thing about the way I was raised, it would be . . .

8. The five things I feel most grateful for are . . .
9. Personal living or work habits I would like to change in myself are . . .
10. How I feel about my own mortality is . . .
11. Three specific things that make you a pleasure to live with are . . .
12. Three specific things that make you difficult to live with are . . .
13. What I am most afraid of is . . .
14. The person I most resent is . . .
15. My feelings about my success in life are . . .
16. My greatest anxieties are . . .
17. An unforgettable evening with you would include . . .
18. A perfect weekend with you would consist of . . .
19. An important change I want to see in myself . . .
20. I got a big spiritual wake-up call when . . .

Heart Talks–Level A: Ambivalences

1. The best thing about our sex life is . . .
2. The worst thing about our sex life is . . .
3. The parts of my body and appearance I dislike the most are . . .
4. The parts of my body and appearance I like the most are . . .
5. A negative behavior pattern I have is . . .
6. A negative behavior pattern I notice in you is . . .
7. The biggest trade-off in my life is . . .
8. The three things I like best about my life are . . .
9. The way I would feel more loved by you is . . .
10. What my "shadow self" looks like is . . .
11. I have ambivalent feeling/thoughts about . . .
12. What are some of the major decisions in your life you would change, if you could?
13. How well do you live up to your moral, spiritual and ethical values?

14. How would you like to be remembered after you die?
15. What aspects of your personality do you regard as weak?
16. What would you be willing to die for?
17. What are your three most treasured memories?
18. When have you felt hatred for someone in your family?
19. Whom else have you ever hated, and why?
20. When did you last cry by yourself and why?
21. What do you really think of my family?
22. If you knew you had only one year to live, what might you do differently?
23. If there were three specific qualities or abilities you would like to see me acquire, what would they be?
24. What would you do if I developed a life-threatening or chronically debilitating illness?
25. Was there a time in your life you had suicidal thoughts? What was going on?

Heart Talks–Level S: Secrets

It is helpful for you to write down your own secret(s) in detail before you consider sharing them in a Heart Talk. Consider the following: What underlies the fear of expressing your secrets? What are you afraid might result? How does this secret(s) reduce your ability to love yourself? What do you hope to gain by hiding or withholding this secret(s)? What is the cost to the relationship of not communicating whatever it is you are afraid to share? How does this secret affect your self-image? What is the worst you imagine your partner might think or do, if you revealed yourself? What is the best your partner might think or do if you revealed yourself?

Generally, when there is a secret, there is an underlying feeling of shame. Shame is the cancer of the spirit. It can erode your peace of mind; dampen your passion and eventually destroy your love relationship. Shame-based secrets whisper in the crevices of your being that you are undeserving, unworthy and perhaps even despicable. Shame can turn intimacy into a sham.

Everyone has felt ashamed at one time or another. Everyone has been humiliated. Everyone has thought he or she is the only one who harbors shameful secrets. Acknowledging and sharing a painful secret can free you.

Explore with your partner, as openly and specifically as possible, from among the following:

1. The three most dishonest, dishonorable things I have ever done are . . .
2. What I feel most ashamed of is . . .
3. The fears and inhibitions I don't want known are…
4. The faults and disabilities I don't want known are…
5. My biggest, darkest secret is…
6. I've been secretly resentful about . . .
7. Two specific things I don't want you to know about me are . . .
8. I harbor hostility over…
9. What were the most embarrassing memories of your adolescence?
10. What actions have you most regretted in your life and why?
11. What experience have you had with illicit drugs?
12. What specific events in your life have been the most traumatic and emotionally painful?
13. Do you have a secret sexual fantasy that you would like to have fulfilled?
14. What outrageous thing might you do sexually, if you were sure no one would judge you?
15. When did you last want to yell at me, and why?
16. What thoughts do you have when you see yourself nude in the mirror?
17. What have been your biggest failures?

18. What have you done that was sinful, unethical or criminal?

Late Night Heart Talks

Some couples prefer to engage in Heart Talks at the end of the day. Partners take turns completing at least one of the following statements:

1. "What I appreciated most about you today is:_____."
The purpose is to share specific feelings, events and observations that contributed in a constructive way to the overall enhancement of the relationship. You acknowledge something positive that your partner said or did during the day.

2. "What I want to acknowledge myself for is: _____."
This exercise allows you to appreciate and reinforce a new habit or achievement. You might also acknowledge yourself for a contribution to the relationship.

These late-night Heart Talks are never for introducing "heavy issues," but rather to connect positively with your partner before going to bed.

An Adventure of the Heart

Married for eight years, Bill and Julia came to one of my relationship seminars. Bill was a corporate vice-president and Julia a city planner. With their three-year-old son enrolled in daycare, they appeared to juggle their two-career household quite successfully.

Opposites attract was the best description of the dating stage of this couple. Julia was emotionally open and spontaneous, while Bill was more restrained and reserved. Julia found stability and security in Bill, who had his feet firmly planted on the ground. Bill found joy and more aliveness in Julia's emotional intensity.

Opposites, however, can not only attract, they can also repel. Eight years later, their marriage had become burdened by resentments and hostility. Julia felt controlled by Bill, who now seemed to not just have his feet on the ground, but encased in cement. To adjust to Bill's emotional unresponsiveness and rigidity, Julia had learned to dampen her passion and desires. As Julia shut down, Bill felt threatened and rejected; he became even more emotionally withdrawn. With mounting frustration and frequent arguments, they started talking of divorce.

Intimacy had become increasingly difficult at a time in their relationship when they needed it most. The following diagram illustrates how Bill and Julia operated with regard to intimacy and self-disclosure:

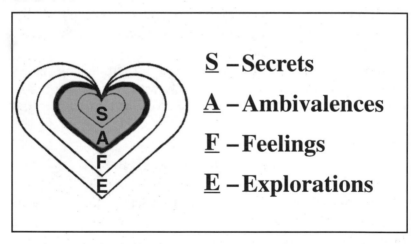

S – **Secrets**

A – **Ambivalences**

F – **Feelings**

E – **Explorations**

Although they communicated at Level E (Explorations) and partially at F (Feelings), neither shared his or her innermost world. Levels A (Ambivalences) and S (Secrets) were almost completely walled off. Bill and Julia had deluded themselves into believing they had a good relationship, when in fact they kept their most intimate thoughts, feelings and desires to themselves. Painful feelings you resist, persist; painful feelings you share can be resolved.

Bill and Julia used Heart Talks to create an environment of emotional safety. They learned that what were once threatening thoughts and feelings dissolved through Heart Talks. Through these regular sessions of self-disclosure, they overcame deep personal fears. They discovered that they could share painful feelings with greater respect and love for each other than ever before.

Heart Talks that Bill and Julia found most revealing were as follows:

Level A: Ambivalences
- What are some of the major decisions in your life you would change, if you could?
- When did you last cry by yourself?
- If there were three specific qualities or abilities you wanted me to acquire, what would they be?

Level S: Secrets
- I've been secretly resentful about . . .
- Two specific things I don't want you to know about me are . . .
- When did you last want to yell at me, and why?

The following is an excerpt from Julia and Bill's first session with Heart Talks:

Julia
"You encouraged me to go back to work in order to help out with expenses and take some of the pressure off you. But now that I'm working full time, you complain that it takes away from the quality time I spend with you and our son. You wanted me to depend on you less and follow my dreams, but it seems that your ambitions are more important.

"Sometimes you say to me, 'Please tell me what's upsetting

you.' Yet when I tell you why I'm angry with you, you say I'm 'just under a lot of stress.' That infuriates me even more!

"When I do make myself available to pamper and please you, I feel taken for granted, or like I'm just complying with your demands. If I take time for me, with yoga classes or going out with business associates, you accuse me of being selfish and rejecting you.

"When I attempt to relate my frustrations about work, you don't listen but go into a monologue about 'harsh realities' and 'office politics,' and how I should now understand what you've been going through.

"You want me to take more sexual initiative and be more passionate. Yet when I try to be sexually assertive, you feel pressured and intimidated. I'm left feeling frustrated and you seem shutdown and bored.

"You still make the rearing of our son my prime responsibility. You get to 'pitch in' by giving him a bath or reading him a story. You act like 'Dr. Child Expert' accusing me of being overprotective and worrying too much about his needs. Why won't you share more of the hands-on parenting and take some of the burden off of me?"

Bill

"You resent having to take prime responsibility for the household, yet I put in longer hours at work and I'm still the one chiefly responsible for our financial support. When I do vacuum or put away the dishes, you get supercritical and say it's easier to do it yourself.

"You encourage me to have male friends, but when I spend a weekend with a fishing buddy, you get jealous. Then I feel guilty for neglecting you and our son.

"You say I should work less, but since you've gone back to work we're also spending more. You think I'm preoccupied with money and my career as a way of avoiding you. That hurts. You want me to be super-successful and yet be completely open and relaxed. Well, you've discovered for yourself that it's not that easy.

"You want me to be more romantic and sensual and less sexually goal-oriented. Yet you wonder what's wrong when I do relax and occasionally lose my erection. You want me to be a great lover 'your way'; I feel confused and manipulated.

"When I want to be nurtured and cared for, you say I'm demanding. I'm reluctant to ask for a backrub or request a special meal. If I don't share my feelings and needs, you say I'm closed off from you. If I do express them, you think I'm selfish and needy.

"I resent that you don't appreciate how much I love our son. You accuse me of having only fun times with him, but no matter what I do, it's never enough. I just can't seem to please you."

Through Heart Talks, these revelations were discussed with care, and gradually resolved. As Julia described, "It felt so good not to have to censor myself, or have to comply just to keep the peace. I feel a new freedom; like I could tell Bill anything I would tell my best friend." With eyes wet, Bill said softly, "I've never felt so vulnerable, and yet not judged by Julia, or anyone else for that matter. I've stopped being so self-critical. Julia and I have gotten to know each other in a deeper way. We no longer walk around on eggshells; our love has gotten stronger."

Renewing Your Love

An intimate relationship must be continually nurtured if it is to thrive. The following practice, which is aptly called "Renewing Your Love," is to remind you of the qualities that attracted you to your partner in the first place.

Sit in silence facing each other, as closely as possible. Close your eyes, breathe slowly and deeply, and relax each part of your body. Tune into yourself and let go of the concerns and cares of the day. Take time to be centered, to feel peaceful and loving. When you and your partner have both opened your eyes, take each other's hands. Look into your partner's eyes lovingly, with an open heart. Keep gazing into the eyes of your partner as you send forth feelings of love. You might also visualize a beam of light pouring down on both of you, and between your hearts. With each breath, the light grows brighter.

Now, bring to mind a specific time when you were powerfully attracted to your partner, when you were deeply and passionately in love. Bask in these beautiful feelings. Continue to breathe deeply as you radiate love through your eyes.

Most importantly, intensify this memory of peace and passion together, until it becomes the experience of your love right now. This peace, intimacy and passion has been there all along, covered over by the superficialities of life. Continue focusing on your feelings of attraction to this wondrous being in front of you.

Breathe out all thoughts of fear and worry. Keep opening your heart and body to peace, passion, yearning and desire. Allow sexual feelings to flow through your entire body. Look deeply into the eyes of your beloved; merge every part of your being with each other.

When you have completed the nonverbal aspect of this practice, have a Heart Talk to share your experience with one another.

The more often you practice "Renewing Your Love," the more likely you are to enjoy a peaceful, passionate relationship. Each time you make significant eye contact, you will trigger all those powerful, loving, happy moments and you can tap into your joy, passion and love. I highly recommend the "Renewing Your Love" exercise before lovemaking, and before you do a Heart Talk. This is among the most powerful exercises that partners can practice. Take the time!

Family Heart Talks

With the enormous pressures faced by the modern family, you must make sure to find time each week just to connect emotionally. Family life can too easily get stuck on a surface level of roles, rules and responsibilities, without renewing emotional sustenance at the core. Weekly family Heart Talks are a way in which parents and children (as young as five years old) can share feelings on equal footing. These meetings can generate a profound and heartfelt experience of family. Heart Talks help each family member to feel respected, appreciated and validated.

The following case demonstrates how Heart Talks can help families. Ron, an engineer, was thirty-six years old when he married Alexis, a thirty-four-year-old interior designer. After the honeymoon, Ron and Alexis moved in together along with Alexis's ten-and fourteen-year-old sons from a previous marriage. Yet within six months after the wedding, their "happy family" was in serious trouble.

Ron described the problem: "I wanted to marry Alexis. That part was easy. Unfortunately, the kids came with the package. From the beginning, they did everything in their power to make life difficult for me. It may have been competition for Alexis's attention, or a way to stay loyal to their father or perhaps they just didn't like me. In any case, after working five, sometimes six days a week, I wanted to relax quietly at home. I like to watch football on Sundays, but when her sons had their friends over, it was so noisy I could barely hear the TV.

"To make matters worse, when I laid down the law, those brats would run crying to their mother. No matter whether they were right or wrong, she defended them. Alexis said I was a bigger baby than the kids were, and accused me of harboring bad feelings toward them. Damn right I did. Those little monsters were driving me crazy, and they knew exactly what they were up to!"

Ron further lamented, "For years I avoided marriage and starting a family because I couldn't imagine being a parent. When I wound up in the role of 'Dad' to Alexis's kids, it was worse than I had ever imagined it could be."

Ron was a self-critical, highly disciplined individual. His behavior appeared to reflect the belief "when you say something once and kids don't listen, start yelling." When he didn't gain immediate cooperation from his stepsons, Ron became angry, to "show them who is boss."

I explained to Ron that running a family is somewhat like running a business. If the principals don't meet regularly, chaos will ensue. Too often when they do meet, it's due to an "emergency" or conflict resulting from poor communication. To avoid such management-by-crisis, regular family meetings are needed to focus on what the kids are doing right, and to clearly communicate expectations and consequences.

At my suggestion, Ron began the first family meeting by addressing both children: "We didn't ask to be thrown together. But because I love your mother and you are her children, nature put us in the same lifeboat. It would have been smart to acknowledge that in the beginning. I'd like to hear your feelings about us having been thrown together." With support from both Alexis and Ron saying "tell me more," the kids talked of their pain from the divorce. They shared anger toward Ron's critical, perfectionist attitude–not like their permissive weekend-at-Disneyland "real dad."

To Ron's credit, he stayed open and receptive throughout the family Heart Talk. He told them he was committed to becoming a better stepparent. Ron concluded the meeting by affirming, "Instead of making life miserable for one another, let's see how each of us can begin to make our family life more satisfying." Ron gave each child and Alexis a big hug.

Creating Cooperation and Support

At the beginning of each of their Family Heart Talks, each person shared two specific things they appreciated about each family member. This helped maintain an atmosphere of love and support. Though conflicts naturally arose, the level of trust and affection grew. Ron became skillful at catching the kids doing something right, and praising them for it.

To improve cooperation in their family, I suggested an additional exercise: "Creating Cooperation." Everyone has preferences about how others should request cooperation. In this exercise, family members are asked to describe the words and actions that make them want to cooperate, and those that make them more likely to resist or rebel.

For instance, Ron began by saying, "I feel more like cooperating when I am asked in a kind, pleasant voice, and there is respect for other things I might be doing. I feel like rebelling when anyone starts by blaming me for something, and makes me feel like I've done something wrong."

Alexis's older son shared the following: "Ron, I feel exactly the same as you do–I'd be more cooperative if I didn't think you were laying a power trip on me. I rebel when you act bossy and growl at me, I get stressed and think you just hate me."

At that family Heart Talk, Ron declared that he was going to work on being more affectionate and less quick-tempered with the boys. He also requested that they tell him directly when they were upset with his actions, rather than complain behind his back to Alexis. The meeting ended on a positive note, with an exchange of laughter and hugs.

Ron saw that when he gently but firmly stated his needs and preferences, the boys cooperated. He discovered it actually took less effort than yelling. Ron described the change in his behavior as a result: "I don't need to blow up and cause the kids to become rebellious and defiant. Instead of playing the tough guy all the time, I'm starting to connect with them in a way that Alexis loves."

At the next meeting, Ron, Alexis and their two sons made a list of chores each would be responsible for. From then on, each weekly Family Heart Talk included discussions of "The agreements I kept this week are . . . ; "The agreements I broke this week are . . . ; "and "The commitments I'm making to do my chores are . . ."

"I Love You, And . . ."

Certain words and phrases can inadvertently cause negative results. When you say to your loved one, "I love you, but . . .," you are actually making a statement which implies, "I won't love you unless you do what I say." On the other hand, if you say, "I love you, and I'd prefer if you would . . . ," you communicate your unconditional love, along with your request or preference.

Let us consider in greater depth the ever-present three-letter word "but." Used automatically, particularly in intimate relationships, this little word "but" can be deceptively destructive. When you are communicating, "I love you, but . . .," you are invalidating your love. Similarly, if you say, "This is true, but . . . ," what you are really implying is that your partner's experience and feelings are not true, or else irrelevant. The word "but" negates everything your partner has said.

Just think how you feel when your partner "agrees with you, but" or "loves you, but." If you simply substitute the word "and" instead, it creates a completely different experience of heart-to-heart communication. For example, "That is true *and* let me share with you my experience of what took place," or "That is valuable feedback, *and* here is how I experienced the same situation." The word "but" creates disagreement and resistance, the word "and" introduces agreement and creates intimate communication.

The following four phrases will transform the power of your intimate communication:

- I love you, and . . .
- I appreciate you, and . . .
- I agree with you, and . . .
- I respect your point-of-view, and . . .

When you use these four phrases, you are affirming love, appreciation and respect for your partner. You are validating his or her point-of-view. You are building rapport and acknowledging communication rather than ignoring, belittling and negating what has just been said. Further, you are creating a bond by which you and your partner can accept difficult situations and acknowledge that you may have differing points of view. These four phases will help you avoid unnecessary conflict, communicate clearly and enjoy great Heart Talks.

Of course, it is not just what you say, but how you say it. You communicate with your partner more gracefully when you maintain an attitude of love and sensitivity to his or her needs. When you are defensive, critical or judgmental, no amount of discussion, and no amount of "and" versus "but," will result in a solution both you and your partner can enjoy.

Just as "I love you, but" causes negative results, so does "But I love you." This commonly heard protest, "But I love you" communicates you feel great love, but does so defensively. You are giving a message of frustration, "Doesn't my love count for something?" Most of us tend to love another the way we wish to feel loved ourselves. Rather than keep insisting "But I love you," it is important to discover how your partner best experiences feeling loved by you.

For many of us, it is not just the words "I love you," but specific actions that communicate love. For example, a husband may say, "I love you, sweetheart" and she responds, "No, you don't! If you did, you would still look at me and touch me lovingly just the way you did when we were dating. You don't bring me little surprises or take me on romantic trips anymore." For the husband to feel hurt and protest "but I do love you" is to miss the communication. In his preoccupation with business, he has forgotten to touch his wife in the special ways that make her feel most loved. Instead of protesting, the husband would benefit more by regularly creating a special "I love you day" for his wife. That could include her favorite flowers, a love poem, a romantic dinner, an overnight stay at a bed-and-breakfast inn, a massage and once again looking into her eyes in that special way. Such intimacy is what his wife needs to re-experience his love, and what he needs to feel acknowledged and admired.

Knowing how to make your partner feel fully loved is a crucial Love Fitness skill. Sit down and have a Heart Talk, asking, "How do you best experience being fully loved? How do you like to be touched, spoken to, looked at? How do you like me to show my love, care and respect?" Be specific. This Heart Talk is a powerful means to rediscover the similarities and differences between how each of you needs to feel loved.

Chapter 4

Heart-to-Heart, Passionate Lovemaking

Kevin: I've been fantasizing about making love with you all day. *[But I'm not aroused now . . . In fact, I hope I can perform.]*

Ann: Me too. I want you so much. *[Not really; I had a stressful, exhausting day at work.]*

Kevin: Let's get under the covers. *[If I'm standing nude, she'll see how flabby I'm getting.]*

Ann: Okay. *[Why doesn't he ever undress me slowly?]*

Kevin: I'll turn the lights down. *[Oh, oh. I should have created a more romantic, intimate setting, candles, soft music, massage oils; but it's too late and I'm tired.]*

Ann: Great. *[I'd better look eager or he'll feel crushed. Why does he always have to be in such a rush? He hasn't even kissed or hugged me.]*

Kevin: I'd really like you to give me oral sex. *[It's okay to be selfish about my needs; that's what all the sex books say.]*

Ann: Sure. *[I'll just get this over with and go to sleep–he'll never change. I'll fantasize about someone who would make love to me seductively.]*

Kevin: M-mm. That's good. *[I should have just gone to sleep. If this doesn't give me an erection, nothing will.]* You really turn me on. *[Thank goodness, I'm hard. I suppose I should pleasure her too, but I really don't feel like it.]*

Ann: *[This is getting tedious. I'd like a little attention myself, but it feels like he's about to come already.]*

Kevin: C'mon up and let's make love. *[I had better get right to it, before I come.]*

Ann: *[I hope I can get excited quickly. I wonder if those Kegel exercises have made a difference–he probably won't notice–because he didn't even mention it when I colored my hair.]*

Kevin: You're so passionate. *[It's too early to ejaculate now. I should count sheep and focus on my checking account.]*

Ann: So are you. *[What's happened to his hard on? Damn. I had better pretend nothing's wrong.]*

Kevin: Sweetheart, you're the best. *[I hope she doesn't think I'm a premature ejaculator. My penis is already shrinking; I have to make her come right now.]*

Ann: (Sighs, moans, shudders.) *[I'll fake it and not hurt his feelings.]*

Kevin: Did you?

Ann: Oh God, yes. That was incredible. Couldn't you feel it? *[He never knows how to satisfy me . . . but I don't want him to think I can't have an orgasm.]*

Kevin: Oh, yes. Was that a multiple?

Ann: I was so gone I couldn't really count.

Kevin: Next time it'll be even wilder. Why are you so quiet?

Ann: I just feel so intimate and close to you. *[What a fiasco.]*

Kevin: Me too. *[He falls asleep.]*

Kevin and Ann could be a couple on *Sex and the City*. What this dialogue demonstrates is a complete lack of authenticity. Lovemaking is best when it is based on honest communication.

What sustains peace and passion after the early attraction is something more sophisticated than seduction and more enduring than showmanship.

Love Fitness can help you create a passionate and fulfilling sexual relationship. This includes learning how to revitalize a sexual relationship that has gone stale. My focus is not on technique (there are enough sex manuals for that) but on imbuing sex with the magic of heart-to-heart communication.

Beyond Sexual Boredom and Fear

First and foremost, sex establishes a bond that helps to ensure the biological survival of the species. Bonding, according to modern science, is the result of high physiological arousal with close physical proximity.

When they first bond, almost every new couple is prone to believe their passion is so strong it will never diminish. Young couples will often assert, "It will never happen to us." Only after they begin to face the stresses of work, children, financial concerns and the many pressures of family life does a rude awakening occur. Sexual desire diminishes under stress, and sexual performance anxiety is prone to increase. Sex is postponed, and taking the initiative becomes tentative.

Who initiates sex more often, you or your partner? This Heart Talk may present you with a major opportunity to restore passion in your lovemaking. Surveys have consistently found that in approximately two-thirds of love relationships, men initiate sex more often than do their wives or girlfriends.

Those couples with equally balanced initiation, or the woman initiating more, reported higher levels of sexual satisfaction for both partners. A key to greater satisfaction in lovemaking is achieving a more balanced initiation. A man may need to become more receptive to his partner's advances and increased initiative. A woman may need to become more assertive, perhaps by making more verbal requests.

For a woman to show more initiative requires an atmosphere of safety and trust. A monogamous sexual relationship presents every couple with a challenge, and an opportunity. On the one hand, daily responsibilities and pressures at work can dampen sexual passion. On the other hand, a secure and exclusive commitment makes possible a heightened sexual passion, through communicating heart-to-heart.

Most people grow up internalizing barriers to heart-to-heart communication. Boys are encouraged to be strong ("take it like a man"), unemotional ("don't cry"), and tough ("don't let anyone push you around"). Girls are convinced by advertising and MTV to be the object of lust and to dress in a sexually provocative fashion.

The pervasiveness of the cyber-porn industry has altered how children learn about sex. Porn gives teens the wrong idea about human sexuality and encourages them to have sex before they are ready.

This behavioral patterning in childhood results in numerous fears associated with sexual self-disclosure. Many men fear that exposing their sensitive, vulnerable sides will cause women to see them as weak-willed. Many women fear being used, abandoned or else being left unsatisfied. Many older men struggle with performance anxiety and a fear of impotence, as natural hormonal levels decline and it takes longer to become aroused. Many older women face an equally anxiety-laden concern–the fear of being less attractive and therefore less sexually desirable.

Some people feel empty or frustrated after a sexual encounter, even with their spouse. Research shows that when men feel like a failure at work, their testosterone levels decline and they are more likely to feel and act like a failure in bed as well. For women, if there is not enough love, and not enough foreplay, it can inhibit their full sexual response.

Sex can be a routine act of fulfilling desire, in which case boredom is inevitable, or it can be a window of spiritual discovery and depths of passion that can last a lifetime. It is only by trusting your partner with intimate feelings that lovemaking can remain a fulfilling adventure.

How Satisfied Are You With Your Sexual Intimacy?

The following assessment will help you and your partner explore and better understand your sexual relationship. Respond to each question with a "yes" or a "no." Bear in mind there are no "right" answers, only feelings and attitudes to be explored. This material is intended to explore beliefs and habits you "bring to bed with you," that can limit your lovemaking.

1. I worry about whether I am pleasing my partner sexually.
2. I wonder if my partner is faking orgasm.
3. I have difficulty "letting go" and experiencing more passion.
4. I feel blamed by my partner for our sexual difficulties.
5. My partner is responsible for our sexual difficulties.
6. I get irritated when my partner is not in the mood to make love.
7. I feel like it is always up to me to seduce or turn on my partner.
8. I wish my partner enjoyed cuddling more.
9. I am afraid of my partner's reaction when I don't want to make love.
10. Sometimes, "out of duty," I submit to sex but later resent my partner for it.
11. The more demanding my partner is, the more I turn off

sexually.

12. Sometimes I think my partner withholds sex to control, manipulate or punish me.
13. I turn off sexually when my partner doesn't show enough sensitivity, care and tenderness.
14. I sometimes feel depressed, angry or alone after sex.
15. Although I would like to experiment with new and different sexual techniques and toys, my partner is unwilling to try them.
16. I am uncomfortable touching my genitals and pleasuring myself during lovemaking.
17. We tend to repeat a sexual routine with regard to foreplay, positions and time of day.
18. During sex, my mind drifts into mundane thoughts.
19. I am troubled by the memory of a negative or painful sexual experience.
20. I have sexual fantasies that I'm too embarrassed to share.
21. I am unsure about the effectiveness of our method of birth control, and worry about getting pregnant.

Remember, each of you is 100 percent responsible for your peace and passion. The more open, honest and specific you are, the greater opportunity you create for sexual intimacy. Review your above "yes" responses while considering the following:

1. I would feel excited by . . .
2. I would feel less pressured if . . .
3. I would love it if you would . . .
4. I specifically want to intensify our lovemaking by . . .

Enhance Your Lovemaking

Here is another quiz that can help you and your partner learn more about one another's sexual concerns and desires. You may find that more than one choice applies to each question. Remember, the issue is not a "right" answer, but rather taking the time to speak intimately about each other's sexual needs and preferences.

1. What you could do to enhance our lovemaking is:
   a. be more spontaneous, playful and creative.
   b. ask what would give me greater sexual pleasure.
   c. express your delight verbally.

2. When I undress in front of you I:
   a. feel upset with the way I look, and get under the covers as fast as I can.
   b. look with scorn at my profile, and make sarcastic comments about my inadequacies.
   c. enjoy being nude.

3. When I share my sexual fantasies with you, I find it:
   a. difficult or uncomfortable.
   b. okay, except for my most secret erotic fantasies.
   c. easy and enjoyable.

4. Lovemaking with you is mostly:
   a. passionate, romantic and loving.
   b. spontaneous, creative.
   c. routine and boring.

5. Oral sex with you is:
   a. uncomfortable and difficult.
   b. a turn-off and repulsive.
   c. exciting and highly pleasurable.

6. When we're making love and you say, "A little slower, please," or "Ouch, please be careful there," I feel:
   a. criticized as a partner.
   b. that I must instantly stop and apologize.

     c. glad that you trust me enough to be outspoken.

7. During intercourse you and I are:
     a. intimately connected.
     b. each in our own thoughts and feelings.
     c. on automatic and engaged in a routine.

8. When we make love, I have an orgasm:
     a. often and easily.
     b. sometimes, with difficulty.
     c. rarely.

9. When I become sexually aroused, it seems you sometimes:
     a. pull back from me by making jokes or changing the subject.
     b. escape by turning on the TV or making something to eat.
     c. withdraw into private thoughts.

10. (For men only) Getting and maintaining an erection:
     a. sometimes causes me anxiety.
     b. is easy, relaxed, something I don't think about.
     c. is a constant fear in the back of my mind.

11. (For women only) When your partner has difficulty achieving or maintaining an erection:
     a. I pretend that it's all right, while wondering what I've done wrong.
     b. I get angry and feel cheated.
     c. I don't feel responsible, but I am supportive.

Just as in the first quiz, take time to share with your partner what you learned about your lovemaking. Were certain issues difficult for you? Which expectations, difficulties or fears regarding sexual intimacy were more pronounced? What in your partner's response surprised you? What in your own response was surprising to your partner?

Sexual Turn-ons and Turn-offs

A couple's intimacy and lovemaking can benefit from discussing the following topics:

- *Fantasy:* Sexual fantasy can dispel boredom and stimulate passion and arousal. You and your partner can use it as a stepping-stone to enhance your love life. Sharing your most intimate fantasies with your partner may require great care and delicacy. You must create a warm, safe environment where any fears that may surface dissolve in love, excitement and pleasure. Remember: just because you disclose a fantasy does not mean you have to act on it.

   Some people are troubled by guilt because of their sexual fantasies. It is quite natural, however, for men and women to have fantasies and often outrageous ones at that. Sexual fantasies are just that; they require neither action nor guilt. Whether fantasies of group sex, homosexuality, extramarital affairs, fetishes or sadomasochism, the only harm is needless shame and fear. One caution: it is important to create an intimate and trusting atmosphere for sharing these fantasies. Disclosing your fantasies without warning or reassurance can arouse jealousy or hostility, harming the relationship.

- *Sex Toys:* Don't be ashamed or embarrassed to add sex toys to your love life. Many women find that a vibrator can add another dimension to sexual pleasure. Those who have had difficulty with their orgasm often find it to be a stimulating and effective tool. Women commonly are concerned that once you use a vibrator that "ordinary lovemaking" won't be the same. Men sometimes express doubts by questioning, "Am I not good enough, why do we need a vibrator?" A vibrator can simply enhance pleasure; it need not become an addiction. With care, it can add variety to your lovemaking.

- *Pornography:* On-Line porn is viewed primarily by males. Most are recreational users who view pornography with curiosity or as a fun diversion. But a new sexual compulsivity unique to the Internet age has emerged. Research has shown that ten percent of men have become addicted to on-line sex and pornography. These men can become so dependent on visual sexual imagery for arousal that their real-life love relationship can become impaired. In such instances, cyber porn can contribute significantly to divorce.

  Some couples, however, report that an occasional erotic video can spark passion and mutual desire. If both partners are agreeable as to content, it can refresh a sex life that has gone stale. If such videos contribute to a heart-to-heart connection as well as erotic stimulation, then they serve a valuable purpose.

- *Medications:* The same line of thinking applies to the use of medical "love potions." Viagra, Levitra and Cialis can treat erectile dysfunction and enhance male performance. Women, like men, can sometimes benefit from taking testosterone to increase sexual desire. Women take it in lower doses than men, in a patch, gel or under-the-tongue formulation. Please see your doctor if a consultation is in order.

Sexual fantasies, erotic videos, vibrators or, if needed, medication, are valuable if they contribute to the high self-esteem of both partners, and to sharing more love.

Can Passion Last?

Kirk is a thirty-one-year-old engineer and Vicky is a twenty-eight-year-old schoolteacher. They were married seven years ago and have two children. With the kids in nursery school and kindergarten, Vicky has gone back to work part-time. From the outside, it appears they have an ideal relationship, with jobs they enjoy, children they love and a bright future.

In a counseling session Kirk complained, "When I come on to Vicky at night, she isn't interested. I don't know what the problem is or what she expects, but withholding sex isn't going to solve anything."

Vicky said, "Kirk always has the same routine; he kisses me, caresses my breasts and then wants intercourse. He usually comes in five minutes or so, and I can't climax that quickly. It's boring and the passion is gone."

Boredom is the principal problem in long-term sexual relationships. "There's no adventure in our lives," Kirk laments. "Every evening is the same. I come home from work exhausted. After dinner we clean up, and put the kids to bed. Then I may have a couple of hours of work to finish. When I go to bed, Vicky is usually asleep. If I awaken her, she's irritated and rarely responds to my sexual overtures. We're in a rut, but I don't know how to get out of it. I wonder if our sex life will ever be passionate again."

Vicky has her own complaints. "Kirk comes to bed past 11:00 P.M. and expects me to be ready and waiting. He hasn't paid any attention to me all day, and isn't sensitive to the fact that I have to get up before he does. He has chores or work he brought home, and there's always some damn sports event he has to watch. When we do have sex, it is mechanical."

Kirk and Vicky are not alone. Millions of young couples are faced with a similar problem. Sociologists have cataloged ad infinitum the cultural forces (rising debt, unrealistic media-driven expectation, the growth of suburbia, the isolation of the nuclear family) that put pressure on marriages. The solution to Kirk and Vicky's problem lies in discovering how they are asphyxiating the magic in their love life.

When Kirk and Vicky came for counseling, I said, "You both realize that you're still in love. The question is whether you are motivated enough to break your negative patterns." Fortunately, they were still optimistic about their relationship. To help them regain the peace, passion and romance they had once enjoyed, I suggested the following exercises:

Acknowledging. Like most couples in conflict, Kirk and Vicky each felt unappreciated. To help remind them of why they were together, I asked them to sit face-to-face, making eye contact as they exchanged acknowledgements. This simple exercise has very few rules. The person speaking describes in one or two specific sentences what he or she appreciates about the person listening. The listener must accept the acknowledgements, saying either "Thank you" or "I got it" after each statement. Next, the listener repeats the acknowledgement as close to the original as possible without adding anything, dodging the compliment or arguing the point.

This exercise was a radical departure from Kirk and Vicky's usual mode of communication, consisting mainly of accusations, demands, threats and counter-threats. A few minutes after Kirk began talking about the things he appreciated about Vicky, both their eyes welled up with tears, and they embraced one another. Neither could deny the love that was underneath the painful conflicts.

Releasing the Flow of Love. Another beneficial exercise was to make a list beginning with the statement: "The ways I've been blocking love in my life is . . ." This technique helps you stop blaming your partner and start seeing how you contribute to the relationship's failure or success. Kirk and Vicky each needed to learn how they had fallen into negative patterns, and how to break out of them.

By honestly recognizing how you contribute to blocking the flow of love, you no longer need attack or blame your partner. It is very important for each partner to take 100 percent responsibility for improving the relationship. Getting stuck in a "poor me" attitude will not get you the results you want. When you are willing to be fully accountable, you are on the road to restoring peace and passion in your relationship.

Having an "A.F.F.A.I.R." with Your Spouse

By acknowledging how each had been stifling their love, Kirk and Vicky created a breakthrough. They felt a great release when recognizing that their sexual problems were not causes, but symptoms of difficulties that they could overcome. This expanded perspective helped them explore other aspects of Love Fitness, to regain the spontaneous affection that first characterized their relationship. In order to further assist Kirk and Vicky restore passion in their relationship, I suggested they have an "A.F.F.A.I.R.":

> **A - Adventure**
> **F - Fun**
> **F - Fantasy**
> **A - Affection**
> **I - Intimacy**
> **R - Romance**

A: Adventure. Kirk and Vicky each wanted to break out of their boring routine. As a result, they set up creative adventure days. At least twice a month, Kirk or Vicky took turns being responsible for a day trip or fun weekend adventure. One weekend, Kirk took Vicky and the kids for rides at a nearby amusement park. Another weekend, Vicky took Kirk on an art tour of museums and galleries he "never had time for." One Sunday, Kirk encouraged Vicky to spend the morning lounging in bed while he and the children made breakfast for her.

One Saturday evening Kirk catered to Vicky's sensual desires rather than focusing on intercourse. I suggested he have her draw a "pleasure map" of her body indicating exactly where she would like to be caressed, stroked, massaged and kissed. Kirk was to be strictly in the role of her grateful, accommodating love slave.

F: Fun. Couples who play together, stay together. Marriage doesn't always have to be "grown-up." All work and no play makes any love relationship dull. You can often increase your energy for problem solving, challenges and responsibilities by taking time to play. Here are some fun suggestions:

1. Have a private party in your bedroom. Cover the bed with rose petals and tie balloons to the bedpost. Wear something sexy, turn on romantic music, dim the lights and pour two glasses of champagne.
2. Create a theme dinner. You could arrange a Japanese setting on your living room floor with two pillows facing each other, some incense, candles, chopsticks, cups of hot sake or tea and take-out sushi. To further enhance the mood, you can wear a robe or kimono you can easily slip off.
3. Experiment with role-playing. For example, have your partner treat you like a young ingénue, innocent and uncertain of what to do; you've never done anything like this before and you feel shy. State the rules: petting is okay, no intercourse, etc. Dress for the part. The point is, break out of the old roles and into the new.

F: Fantasy. Allow yourselves the freedom to act out a safe fantasy, giving your imagination and creativity free reign. Take turns or else create the fantasy together. Consider the following questions:

- What kind of character would you/your partner be?
- What place, time, period and setting would you find

yourselves in?
- What kind of life would you lead?
- What romantic and/or sexual fantasy would your characters play out?

This exercise is not only fun but also revealing. It allows partners to explore each other's dreams and fantasies. You might consider indulging your fantasies for an hour or even the entire day, using costumes and props. Be theatrical. Here is how some couples have used their imagination:

- You go back to the time you met and the first time(s) you made love.
- You imagine playing the courtesan and the conqueror.
- You have entered a palace of sexual pleasure with a personal love slave at your beck and call.
- You each write an erotic fantasy and then read it to one another.

A: Affection. There is nothing more welcome, when you're feeling down, than a hug from your partner. In every relationship there will be occasions when one partner needs more from the other and vice versa. Be sensitive to those times with considerate, loving gestures. Love blossoms when care is rendered and affection is communicated. For example, write your partner a poem, give a foot rub, or wash and comb each other's hair.

Try the following Heart-to-Heart exercise without speaking. Close your eyes, take a deep breath, and let go of the day's tension as you exhale and relax your entire body. Continue breathing in this way until you feel quite relaxed. Next, one partner rests their hands on the other partner's heart; feel it pulsating with life and energy. Be receptive to everything the heart is conveying and remain open and silent, simply receiving, for three minutes. Then have your partner do the same for you, holding his or her hands over your heart for three minutes. Next take turns sharing what each of you was feeling.

I: **Intimacy.** Intimacy means "into-me-see." Let your partner see into you, and assist your partner to feel safe enough to let you see into him or her. It is especially important to communicate your feelings during lovemaking. Don't be afraid of simple direct statements such as, "I like it when you…" "It turns me on when you let me…" "I would like it if you would …more" "I get uncomfortable when you …" Expressing your feelings increases trust and gives permission to expand the pleasures of your lovemaking.

Compose a list of the most intimate questions you would like your partner to answer. For example: How does it feel when I reach orgasm with you? Is there a way in which you feel I could be more sensitive during lovemaking? Are you happy with how I touch you?

Be willing to share your deepest feeling and fears around lovemaking:
- "I'm frightened of being too close to you, I'm afraid I might lose myself."
- "I don't want you to become bored with me."
- "I am not interested in sex right now but would like you to hold me."
- "I feel like you tune me out when we are making love."
- "I fear you can't accept my bodily imperfections."
- "I like it when you don't expect or need an orgasm."
- "I'm afraid I can never satisfy you."

R: Romance. You must continue to fan the flames to keep romance alive, in a long-term relationship. True romance includes a seduction of spirit. Here are some ideas:

1. Imagine a romantic evening. What would make it special,

memorable, unique? What would you wear and eat? What music and sights might you fill your environment with? Now actually follow through and make it happen.

2. Romance does not have to cost you anything–a romantic gesture can be a love letter, a wildflower, a walk by the seashore. Be tourists in your own city, guests in your own home.

3. Give yourself the freedom to be apart. Absence does make the heart grow fonder. Some couples stifle romance with constant togetherness. By being apart, you give yourselves room to grow, and then later to discover each other anew.

While it seems obvious, it must be said: by far the most import element for fulfilling sex is love. The more fully you and your partner feel a strong connection, the better your lovemaking will be. The key to solving sexual difficulties may be to first learn to relax deeply. From that foundation of inner peace you can be more playful and naturally rekindle the spark.

Remember, the great adventure of intimate sex is inward, a journey of the heart and soul as well as the senses. Your spirits can leap free of worn-out roles and misbeliefs to experience the deep joy of renewal and letting go. Lovemaking can then become a profound spiritual experience of union and bliss.

Chapter 5

Working Out Anger And Getting Close

AN IRONY OF LOVE is that it guarantees conflict and anger. When two people fall in love, they expose the most sensitive parts of their personalities. At some time in every love relationship, partners are inconsiderate, hurt each other's feelings or let each other down. Hurt and anger is the natural result, and to keep love vibrant, these feelings must be appropriately expressed. The closer you are to someone, the more adept you must be at communicating hurt and anger constructively. This chapter represents key Love Fitness workouts to help you transform anger from a destructive problem into an opportunity for intense communication, more mutual respect and, ultimately, deeper love.

No one enjoys being a target of another's anger, especially that of a love partner. A peak level of Love Fitness is to maintain inner peace and soothe your emotions, even in the midst of an argument. Can you recall a recent incident in which your partner became angry with you? How did you respond? Were you able to keep your emotional equanimity? Was the situation fully resolved, or were you swallowing your feelings?

Jim, a client, recounted a Sunday-morning exchange with his live-in girlfriend, Donna:

Donna: Oh, Jim, you did it again! You took a shower and now the floor is soaking wet.

Jim: Well, you forgot to put the cap back on the toothpaste; it oozed out onto the counter.

Donna: You left the cap off, not me.

Jim: Gimme a break. I work so hard. Can't I even take a shower in peace?

Donna [gritting her teeth]: Okay, honey, just do what you want.

Jim: Geez, why do you always get to be "right"? You are always bitching at me. I can't even relax in my own home because of all the hostility.

Donna: You never listen to me; you keep trying to intimidate me.

Jim: Me, intimidate you?

Donna: Yes. You never let me finish a sentence. Every time I start to say something, you jump right in and–

Jim: That's not true!

Donna: There you go again.

Jim: Okay, go ahead, say whatever it is you need to say.

Donna: I'm tired of cleaning up after you–why can't you be more conscious of the extra work you create for me?

Jim: Hey, you make it sound as if I'm a pig! Can I help it if you are a compulsive nut about sterilizing the bathroom?

Donna: Ah, forget it. You'll never change.

Sound familiar? How many times have you and your partner found yourselves quarreling over something so minor you later forgot why you were arguing? How much bickering, hostile silence or insomnia did it take before you finally made up?

In most relationships, anger erupts and subsides with few, if any, positive results. There is no appropriate exchange of feelings beyond heated words and defensive responses. No one has learned what must change in the relationship to avoid future emotional explosions. Feelings are not fully resolved, nor is there a convergence of points of view. Instead of using the energy of anger to deepen heart-to-heart communication, most couples find that anger outbreaks leave them emotionally bruised and resentful. They rely on time to do the healing and hope that the angry outburst will eventually blow over. The tragedy, however, is that this approach ultimately leads to emotional distance and the erosion of passion. It slowly poisons love.

Managing Anger

In itself, anger is not a problem; it's what you do or fail to do with the anger that can result in a breach of your love relationship. When anger is misdirected, turned inward or used as ammunition, it can initiate a destructive and hostile interchange. When anger is accepted–that is, experienced, identified and managed well–it can provide the power to solve the inevitable conflicts that arise in a love relationship.

Elise and Hunter sought help near the end of their first year of marriage. "Before we were married," Elise lamented, "Hunter was so thoughtful. We compromised a lot. He really listened to me. Now, it's all changed. Everything has to go his way all the time!" Hunter's point of view was quite different. "I don't know what she's so upset about. Our relationship is great. There's no reason for us to be here except that she's become so damn cold. I can't understand it."

Elise and Hunter had a common problem. Once they got married, Hunter became more absorbed in the pressures of his career and less attentive to Elise's feelings. Elise, however, had never before experienced Hunter's lack of sensitivity towards her. Now she was shocked, disappointed and confused about how to reach him emotionally.

Elise was clearly hurt but was unable to express her anger. I explained that to manage her feelings of anger effectively, it was important for her to understand that anger could have a positive purpose. Quite often, couples hurt one another without malicious intention. That is why Hunter responded to Elise's cold silence with the question, "Why are you so upset?"

When you get angry, your body and mind are giving you a signal that you feel hurt and pain. Whether you feel ignored, unappreciated, manipulated, wronged, put down or controlled by your partner, the common denominator is pain and hurt.

Anger is a natural response to feeling hurt, just as fire is the natural result of applying intense heat to wood. Once Elise realized that underneath her anger she was hurt, and that underneath her hurt was pain, she recognized why expressing her anger was so important. Healthy anger communicates the hurt, releases the pain and unblocks the underlying love.

I also helped Elise to understand how anger could empower her to communicate more effectively with Hunter and break through his seeming insensitivity. When you get angry with your partner, you are saying, "Stop! I feel hurt!" Elise, like so many women, had denied herself the freedom of such intense, direct communication because she had a habit of internalizing anger. Elise needed to feel her anger and then mange it constructively.

Elise was able to become more assertive as she grew more comfortable with channeling her anger. When you feel hurt by your partner, the initial response is often shock. Elise initially felt both shaken and powerless in the face of Hunter's self-centered withdrawal. Repeated hurts not acted upon can make you feel helpless, small and powerless. The emotional energy of anger surging through your body is empowering. Anger is nature's way of giving you back your strength when your partner has intentionally or unintentionally caused you pain.

Elise and Hunter worked with the Love Fitness workouts described in this chapter to deal more constructively with their hurt and anger. In particular, I encouraged them to talk about each other's anger styles. Hunter learned that Elise's cold withdrawal was not a rejection of him but her response to hurt. He learned to "read" her anger and to encourage her to express her hurt feelings and needs. They soon understood that anger could be a welcome, if sharp signal that heart-to-heart communication is needed.

Making anger work is a great challenge for many couples. Healthy anger requires skill and courage; you must be committed to "work out" feelings with your partner rather than surrender to negative emotional habits. Essential to the Love Fitness program is using each argument as an opportunity to create more mutual respect and greater dignity. The key is to express anger appropriately with constructive and clear communication.

Quiz: How Do You Handle Anger?

Most people did not grow up in households where they watched their parents express or receive anger in ways that strengthened their love. On the contrary, anger is such a difficult emotion that few adults have learned how to manage it well.

Here is a quiz to help identify you and your partner's anger styles. First, review the list and mark each statement that applies to you with your first initial. Next, review the list again and mark each statement that you feel applies to your partner with his or her first initial.

The way that I/you deal with anger is as follows:

1. Bottle up frustration until there's a volcanic explosion.
2. Withdraw and start to cry.
3. Stonewall or deny it; "Angry, who me?"
4. Smile on the outside, and try to cover up the anger.
5. Displace or redirect anger to a child, other people or pet.
6. Swallow the anger and release it through physical symptoms such as headache, ulcers or fatigue.
7. Release the energy of the anger by going out for a run, or with another physical outlet.
8. Use prayer or meditation to suppress the anger rather than release it.
9. Threaten to pack up and leave.
10. Become emotionally distant and bitter.
11. Discuss the upset and see how better to deal with the situation now and in the future.
12. Try to make you feel guilty, wrong or bad for being angry.
13. Give in for fear of becoming enraged.
14. Listen receptively until a solution can be found.
15. Become sad and depressed.
16. Become tense and nervous.
17. Argue vehemently, badger to get compliance.
18. Attack the other's position as being stupid, misinformed or incompetent.
19. Withdraw, sigh or sulk until your partner apologizes.
20. Avoid any upset to keep the peace.
21. Try to cheer you up as soon as you get angry.
22. Tell you in detail about a similar problem I once had, saying, "It's nothing to be angry about, don't feel bad."
23. Listen attentively and empathically.
24. Say, "It's your problem so don't bother me."
25. Overeat, drink alcohol or use drugs.
26. Say, "You're crazy; you should see a therapist."
27. Try to win the argument at all costs, just to be "victorious."

28. Threaten to expose your behavior to family and friends.
29. Shame the other person for "snarling and showing their teeth."

For each item you marked with an initial, explain your choices to your partner. Don't analyze whether a response is right or wrong, good or bad. The purpose of this quiz is to help you understand how you each deal with anger. This exercise is for you and your partner to gain valuable feedback. Please remember, you do not have to agree on how you perceive each other's anger styles.

Constructive Versus Destructive Anger

Now that you have an understanding of how you and your partner cope with anger, you can begin expressing it more effectively. Use these questions to evaluate the anger style you've identified above. Anger is more likely to be received constructively when you can answer "yes" to each of the following five questions:

1. Does my response help my partner feel safe?
2. Does my response call immediate attention to a specific problem?
3. Does my response release hurt and pain, and unblock the love?
4. Does my response communicate a need for a specific behavior change?
5. Does my response affirm feelings of dignity and self-worth?

Answering "yes" to all five questions indicates you express anger in healthy, appropriate ways. Anger is a difficult emotion to master in love relationships because so many of us incorrectly believe that anger and love are incompatible.

Because anger is of necessity a forceful emotion, it can very easily be destructive to a love relationship. Take heart. You can transform anger into a positive force in your relationship. Fundamentally, anger takes two directions: constructive or destructive. Your intention, to appropriately communicate your hurt or to merely strike back with a vengeance, is critical. This intention is subtle and can be easily overlooked amidst the surging adrenaline that accompanies anger. How you shape your intention at the earliest moments of feeling anger, constructively or destructively, is absolutely critical.

If your intention is merely to strike back, then your anger is almost inevitably destructive. Whether you scream at the top of your lungs or sulk in cold silence, the goal remains the same–vengeance and retaliation. You explode in rage to punish your partner for the hurt he or she caused you. Your anger spurs hostility and bitterness and freezes the relationship in negative events from the past. You wind up trying to put down or manipulate your partner, while the positive goal of expressing your hurt is left undone.

In contrast, if your intention is to communicate your hurt and be assertive, your anger can be constructive. This intention makes anger supportive and imbues your expressions of anger with a commitment to a positive outcome. You assertively communicate your hurt feelings and explain what specific change you need. Your anger releases tension and facilitates an emotional breakthrough that helps your relationship rise to a new level of mutual understanding. Consider the following characteristics of destructive versus constructive anger:

Destructive Anger

Destructive anger is a self-fulfilling prophecy in which anger begets anger. It involves the following elements:

1. Manipulative comments to coerce your partner: "If you loved me, you would . . ." "If you don't like it, leave." "Do what you want, but don't come crying to me."

2. A lengthy monologue to try to control and dominate: "Let me finish, I've got more to get off my chest." "I don't want to hear your excuses." "You'll just have to wait."

3. All-encompassing accusations that use words such as "never," "always," "should" and "ought." For example: "You *never* listen." "You always do this to me." "You *should* be more considerate." "You *ought* to know better."

4. An attempt to make your partner wrong and guilty: "You know how much I count on you; this shows you don't really care." "You're a fool; after all that I've done for you." "How can you be so selfish?"

5. An uncontrolled outburst of anger, yelling to intimidate your partner: "Look at what you've done now." "This is the last straw." "I hate you."

6. The use of old resentments as ammunition: "This is just like the time you . . ." "You're just like your mother." "You've always been that way."

7. The use of emotional blackmail, playing the martyr: "This hurts me more than it hurts you." "I am wasting my breath talking to you." Sighs and moans signaling "Poor me."

Caution: Alcohol is the number one precipitant of family violence and destructive anger. For the susceptible individual, or if a relationship is fragile, even "a couple of drinks" can increase the likelihood of destructive arguments. If there is any indication of alcohol abuse or alcoholism, please contact your physician, and consider Alcoholics Anonymous and Alanon.

Constructive Anger

Constructive anger is committed to a positive outcome and is shaped by the following characteristics:

1. Gets immediate attention through assertive but warm statements: "We've got to talk now, I'm angry . . ." "I'm upset and need to explain why . . ." "I'm hurting; please give me your best attention."

2. Communicates hurt feelings using "I" statements: "I feel let down and very disappointed..." "I feel rejected when..." "I resent that..."

3. Conveys a specific request for change: "Please call me, if you are going to be more than twenty minutes late. . ." "I felt ignored at the party. Next time, I'd like to be introduced to your associates."

4. Leaves you open to your partner's feelings and point of view: "I can see how you feel." "I now understand our miscommunication. What can we do to avoid this problem in the future?"

5. Empowers both partners to change a negative pattern through mutual cooperation: "Since we both want . . we'll need to watch for . . ." "What can we have done differently?" "If we remember to each say, 'Tell me more,' we'll do better."

6. Shows patience while expecting a determined effort to change: "I want you to stop nagging me, but I know it's going to take time." "It's normal to have some ups and downs, and we must . . ." "I know you're trying and I appreciate it; what more can we do to really solve this problem?"

7. Prepares the emotional ground for forgiveness and moving forward: "I love you, and what we need to work on is . . ." "I value and respect you greatly and that includes your ability to discuss this difficult matter."

Shaping anger with constructive characteristics isn't always easy. Sharing anger constructively must not leave you feeling that your anger is bottled up. The heat and hurt must be released.

Practice is crucial. Anger becomes intimate when you express it with the following elements:

1. *Care.* You draw attention to how you've been hurt, but do so with care.
2. *Specificity.* You communicate what specifically caused your hurt.
3. *Release.* You effectively and safely release the pain and hurt that accompanies your anger so you can heal and forgive.
4. *Brevity.* You avoid lengthy monologues. Although an issue may need further examination, you express your feelings succinctly.
5. *Fairness.* You avoid all-encompassing accusations. You recognize that your partner may have an explanation, disagreement or grievance. You remember that when it comes to feelings, no one is wrong.
6. *Receptivity.* You avoid blaming, attacking or otherwise trying to control your partner's responses. This means listening receptively and empathically to your partner's anger without becoming defensive.
7. *Creativity.* You seek to resolve the issues that are confronting you so that, if possible, you both can win. Constructive anger mobilizes you to find mutually satisfying solutions, multiple options and creative choices.
8. *Love.* You are committed to the relationship. You speak from your heart in a way that reflects your pain but also your love.

The Repetition Exercise: Dissolving Anger

The "Repetition Exercise" is a tool to resolve hurt feelings and ease tension between you and your partner.

Jean and Daniel were married for three years. Both were in their mid-thirties. Daniel was an architect, and Jean trained show horses. Both were so involved in their careers that they sometimes went for days without intimate communication. When destructive bouts of anger began to threaten their marriage, Jean insisted they seek help. Their crisis involved conflicting visions of their future. Daniel wanted children, and a wife who would be a full-time homemaker. Jean was committed to her career, and ambivalent about having children.

When Daniel tried to explain why he wanted to start a family as soon as possible, Jean was too preoccupied with her fears to listen attentively. It was the same with Daniel when Jean spoke. They resorted to below-the-belt personal attacks because neither felt the other was willing to listen or "give in." Their bitter arguments led to feelings of betrayal and hostility. These yelling matches escalated, and threats of divorce ensued.

The first question for a couple in crisis is how committed are they to staying together and working things through. Despite the festering hostility, Daniel and Jean said they still loved each other and wanted to make their relationship work. The fact that they came for help together was a healthy sign of their commitment. They needed a specific exercise to practice constructive anger. I coached them in the following "Repetition Exercise":

1. Set aside at least half an hour free of interruptions. Turn off your telephone ringers. Unless there is an emergency, partners agree to practice the Repetition Exercise for as long as necessary for each partner to feel a resolution.
2. Each person begins by affirming his or her commitment to love and to reaching a positive outcome by stating, "Out of the love I have for you, and out of the love I know you have for me, there are some difficult feelings I need to share."
3. Face each other in an open body position, giving each other

your undivided attention. One person speaks at a time, without any interruption.

4. Both partners do their best to maintain eye contact, stay relaxed and create an atmosphere of safety and trust.

5. After your partner speaks, you must accurately restate what he or she said without judging, defending or adding your own interpretation. This requires active, attentive listening. Repetition dissolves tension, creates connection and produces empathy. If you misunderstand, you can ask your partner to "Please repeat."

6. Each feeling or issue must be delivered in no more than two sentences. Communication is specific and non-judgmental. Words like "always," "never," "should" and "ought" are to be avoided.

7. You don't have to agree with what your partner says in order to repeat the communication. The object is to not only repeat the words but to suspend judgment and experience his or her point of view.

8. After repeating the first partner's feelings and points of view, switch roles. You now have a chance to be the speaker. Remember, you can say only two sentences at a time. Your partner repeats back what you have said, without adding any comments of their own. The process continues until your anger has been fully expressed, heard and dissolved. At the end of this exercise, share a hug and say, "I love you." Remember, one of the greatest gifts you can give someone you love is to hear his or her anger and frustration without judging, contradicting or becoming defensive.

Daniel and Jean carefully reviewed the characteristics of constructive anger (described earlier). Daniel told Jean that he strongly desired children, and reminded her of their agreement to start a family when they got married. Daniel explained how upset he was, and Jean repeated each statement back to him. At first, Jean felt uncomfortable repeating Daniel's lines, since it was his anger that she had been resisting. She listened without interruption and repeated Daniel's statements without any judgments or interpretation. Jean was careful to avoid any wisecracks or snide comments. While she had much to say, she knew she would have her opportunity to do so later.

Here is a summary of Daniel and Jean's initial "Repetition Exercise."

Daniel: Out of the love I have for you, and out of the love I know you have for me, there are some difficult feelings I need to share.

Jean [repeats his sentence]: Out of the love you have for me and out of the love you know I have for you, there are some difficult feelings you need to share.

Daniel: I am furious that you keep refusing to have a child. Your, and therefore our, biological clock is ticking away.

Jean: You are furious I keep refusing to have a child. My, and therefore our, biological clock is ticking away.

Daniel: I feel betrayed–you and I had an agreement to start a family when we first got married.

Jean: You feel betrayed–you and I had an agreement to start a family when we first got married.

Daniel: I hate your show horses; I can't believe they mean more to you than having a child.

Jean: You hate [pauses] my show horses. You think they mean much more to me than having a child.

Daniel: I am scared that when you're finally ready to get pregnant, it'll be too late.

Jean: [Repeats]

Daniel: I feel like we've both been exploding with anger; I'm scared we're going to break up.

Jean: [Repeats; tears are flowing.]

Daniel: It hurts me to see you so upset.

Jean: [Repeats}

Daniel: I love you very much. I hope we can work this out. I appreciate your listening; I feel relief.

Jean: [Repeats]

SWITCH: Daniel and Jean now switch roles.

Jean: Out of the love I have for you, and out of the love you have for me, there are some difficult feelings I need to share.

Daniel: [Repeats]

Jean: I am fed up with how you bully and push me around all the time.

Daniel: You are fed up with being pushed . . . Please repeat.

[Jean repeats her previous statement.]

Daniel: You are fed up with how I bully and push you around all the time.

Jean: I hate when you start pushing and won't let up.

Daniel: You hate when I start pushing and won't let up.

Jean: I hate when you don't listen to my fears and concerns.

Daniel: [Repeats]

Jean: When you panic and yell, I don't feel safe discussing my reservations about having a child.

Daniel: [Repeats]

Jean: I'm the one who would be pregnant, and be the primary caregiver, not you.

Daniel: [Repeats]

Jean: I want us to be very realistic; I'm terrified I'll have all the headaches and responsibilities, while you run free.

Daniel: [Repeats]

Jean: I'm angry that you resent my show horses.

Daniel: [Repeats]

Jean: I want us to be able to talk like this without freaking out.

Daniel: [Repeats]

Jean: I'm scared I may be too old and set in my ways to start raising a child.

Daniel: [Repeats]

Jean: I'm scared that if we have a child, you won't honor and support me in my horse business.

Daniel: [Repeats]

Jean: I've been so worried; I don't want to lose you.

Daniel: [Repeats]

Daniel and Jean completed the "Repetition Exercise" with a warm embrace, declaring, "I love you." After further "Repetition Exercises" and many Heart Talks, they decided that both their needs could be met within the relationship. Jean agreed to have a child; Daniel committed to being equally active as a parent, and to fully support her career. They recognized the need for careful planning and closer communication to make their decisions work.

Once the conflict was moved from the arena of antagonism and misunderstanding to empathy and planning, it stopped being a source of hostility and became an opportunity for Daniel and Jean to grow together. Learning to express intimate anger through the "Repetition Exercise" empowered Daniel and Jean to solve problems that had seemed insurmountable. Since then, they have had two children. Although they have had their challenges, they are closer and happier than ever.

Avoiding "Anger Traps"

Many arguments have little to do with the actual issues or ideas being discussed. For instance, you and your love partner may quarrel over finances, disciplining the children, politics, home remodeling, or even your reactions to a recent film. The anger and heated words of an argument are often less about the issues at hand and more often about the frustration that ensues from not feeling heard. The failure to listen to each other's feelings and acknowledge one another's point of view only exacerbates a difficult situation. I have identified four maladaptive communication habits, called "Anger Traps," that are a frequent cause of problems:

1. Curb your need to be right. Human beings can be incredibly self-righteous. In an argument, it is easy to know how right you are and how wrong the other person is. Both sides feel misunderstood and neither side is willing to relent.

When both partners are defending "I'm right, you're wrong" positions, a simple discussion of a specific issue can evolve into a powerful struggle of wills. You may think you are arguing the merits of an issue, but you wind up responding emotionally as if you were fighting for the survival of your dignity and self-worth.

If you felt dominated in previous relationships, you may have entered this one determined to have you way. Trying to "win" when you and your partner disagree is futile. Fierce competition usually leads to both of you losing, because of diminished affection and the tendency of the "loser" to want to win even more the next time. Most disagreements have to do with priorities, choices, values, and opinions, for which there are no absolute standards of right or wrong.

If you find yourself in a dispute with your partner, try to aim for a resolution in which both of you win, both of you are right, and to the greatest extent possible, both of your needs are fulfilled. Learn to accept reasonable criticism without becoming defensive or vengeful. Don't argue, try to justify your actions, or respond immediately with a criticism or your own. The more you resist listening, the more your partner will persist in telling you what you don't want to hear.

2. *Don't be demanding.* A love relationship that's built upon

"shoulds" and "have tos" feels like a prison of endless demands and duties. When you burden your love partner with "shoulds" you create resistance and resentment. You slowly extinguish the personal freedom that is fundamental to creating peace and passion. Learning to say "I would prefer it if" instead of "You should," and "It would be nice if" as opposed to "You have to", is critical to encouraging your love partner to genuinely meet your needs.

When it comes to beliefs and perceptions, there are multiple right answers. Compromise is necessary and valuable, and ought not to be seen as a sacrifice of a high moral position or standard of perfection. The more you incorporate words such as "sometimes" or "often" and avoid terms such as "never" or "always," the more you and your partner will be served. For a love relationship to thrive, it is best for each partner to feel as if there are about ninety percent "want tos" and less than ten percents "shoulds" and "have tos."

3. *Be less judgmental*. In many cases, anger is triggered by a negative judgment. You can prevent arguments by learning to communicate in less-judgmental ways.

Our thoughts–especially judgments–tend to isolate us and increase distress, whereas our feelings tend to help connect us to others. Thoughts connect our heads, feelings join our hearts. That's because thoughts are more likely than feelings to be heard as criticisms. "I think you're wrong" puts the other person in the position of feeling verbally attacked. As soon as we feel criticized the walls go up and it becomes difficult to hear anything else being said.

If you communicate feelings such as "I feel hurt by what happened" or "I feel upset by what you just said" you are less likely to be perceived as attacking. When your partner is upset, try to put yourself in his or her place and ask yourself, "Why does he/she feel this way? What made him/her behave this way? What can I do to convey love and understanding right now?"

An angry statement that begins with "you" often makes the

listener feel judged or attacked and they feel defensive. An "I" statements is much more likely to be received constructively. Most if not all "you" statements are really camouflaged "I" statements. "You are selfish" really means "I think that you are being selfish in this situation." Statements that being with "you" make it easy to blame the other person, ignoring your own responsibility in the situation. For example, "You should be more affectionate" sounds as if there is something wrong with your partner. On the other hand, saying "I wish that sometimes you could be more affectionate" makes it clear that you are requesting something you need, as opposed to making a personal attack.

4. *Beware of Making Assumptions*. Based on your past experiences, it is only natural to make assumptions about what your partner is thinking or feeling. But you can easily be wrong. Most important, it is unreasonable, and a breech of trust, to contradict what your love partner says he or she is feeling. The solution is simple. Ask what your partner is feeling and accept their report as true.

Freeing yourself of assumptions and judgments allows you and your love partner to see each other anew; fresh in each new moment. You are able to give each other undivided attention, because you don't stay stuck in mental chatter. With "clear reception" you can not only avoid unnecessary anger, but be more fully in the present where love can truly thrive.

Become an Anger A.C.E.

Anger is often incredibly fast and furious. We're primed to accuse or deny, blame or feel victimized. Anger, unchecked, can be volatile and potentially harmful. People say and do things they later regret. Yet the effect of these words and hurtful actions can not always be undone or easily erased by simply saying "I'm sorry."

Chances are, when you're upset, you tell yourself, "I'm angry *because* my love partner made a critical remark" or "I'm angry *because* my husband/wife doesn't spend enough time with me." The problem is that automatic comments such as these set the blame for feeling angry on someone or something *outside* yourself. This perception forces you to wait to feel better until some outside event happens, or someone else changes.

When you blame some*one* or some*thing* else for how you're feeling, you give this person or thing the power to cause your emotional state. In contrast, if at the first moment you feel yourself getting upset or angry, you *pause for five seconds* (you may literally count from one to five if you like)–without saying a word, to recognized this and take full responsibility for how you feel and respond–it's easier to see how many choices you have, and to realize that you can choose not to feel like a victim of outside circumstances. Transforming your anger requires expressing yourself while preserving and nurturing your love relationship, rather than arguing and attacking each other.

For some people, acronyms are helpful devices to remember specific skills under pressure. Here's a useful acronym for recalling constructive anger-management skills whenever you feel the first rush of anger:

A. Assess Accurately
C. Choose Constructively
E. Express Effectively

A. *Assess Accurately:* Especially with a loved one, it's easy to assume inaccurately that he or she is angry. Instead, your love partner may be rushed and tense due to the pressures of school or work, or accumulated daily hassles. He or she may be anxious or short-tempered because they are stressed-out. Ask clarifying questions, such as "I'm sensing that things are tense for you right now, is that right?" "Are you upset with *me* about something? Or is it work . . . or school . . . or . . .?" It's important to be able to quickly and readily distinguish between everyday stress-related "baggage" and genuine interpersonal anger, and to avoid assuming that your loved one *intends* to ignore you or snap at you because of anger at something *you've* done or haven't done. Unfortunately, if you fail to assess things accurately and jump to the conclusion that there's a fight already under way, or keep pressing this person for what he or she simply cannot give right then, your pressure itself can be hurtful and trigger an angry reaction. Your assumption then becomes a self-fulfilling prophecy.

C. *Choose Constructively*: Don't say, "Why are you *always* . . .?" or "There you go, getting angry again!" Rather say, "Did something at work make you late for . . .?" Don't say, "That's an ugly, cheap-looking outfit." Rather say, "You are a handsome man (or great-looking woman), and *I* don't happen to like this outfit on you." Don't say, "Get off my back–I hate your guts!" Rather say, "Right now I'm really feeling (upset, stressed, worried) and I'm getting (or I'm not) angry at *you*."

E. *Express Effectively*: Stop for a moment whenever you feel a surge of anger and ask yourself, "Why am I starting to feel angry, and what, specifically, do I want to change?" Rather than being "right" (and the other person "wrong"), you must be committed to being *effective*. Ask yourself, "How can I best express my anger to get the results I/we want?" Remember, it's essential to be *specific*. For example: "You keep promising to come home for dinner at seven, but it's been seven-thirty or eight five days this past week. Not once did you call to let me know you'd be late. It makes me feel like you don't care, and that hurts, I'm angry." It would have done no good to say, "You make me furious because you're *always* late. You're selfish and don't love me!" Effective anger management asks for an acknowledgment of your hurt and a commitment to avoid the same frustrations in the future.

Becoming an anger *A.C.E.* is not a competition. Instead, the goal is to make anger safe. It is for you and your love partner to learn more about each other, meet each other's needs, and affirm your bond by working out conflicts *together*. This requires skill in expressing your own anger and also acceptance of your loved one's anger as well. Acknowledge and reaffirm each other's efforts to clarify irritations and manage anger effectively. Remember, becoming an anger A.C.E. takes patience and practice.

Chapter 6

Healing the Hurts of Love

THE WOUNDS OF LOVE can heal slowly if left untreated. These hurts, from both childhood and adult relationships, can develop into emotional abscesses and scars that impair the ability to love and be loved. The hurt caused by rejection, shame, betrayal, neglect and loss can sometimes be more disabling than that caused by physical injury.

Hidden Resentments

Denial is a natural response to the hurts of love. The mind automatically responds to intense emotional pain by trying to numb and shut off feelings. Couples often mistakenly deny their hurt feelings with the hope of maintaining stability in their relationship. The result is an accumulation of hidden pain and resentment that adds substantially to the normal tensions of living together. For many, denial works so effectively that they are not aware of how hidden resentments are disabling their ability to love and feel loved. The following are the warning signs of hidden resentments; check off the ones which might apply to you:

- You explode in rage over small matters and later regret what you said.
- You feel left out, overlooked, unappreciated or taken for granted.
- You suffer frequent head, neck, back and stomachaches, or other physical complaints, without a diagnosed medical disorder.
- You regularly poke fun at, make spiteful comments to, and feel like telling off or getting back at those you love.
- You abuse alcohol or drugs, or go on eating binges, when you are emotionally upset.
- You lack confidence in your ability to sustain an intimate relationship.
- You are uncomfortable with aspects of your sexuality.
- You suffer from fears of rejection, disapproval or abandonment.
- You create an "arm's-length-only" intimacy, for fear of being trapped in a committed love relationship.
- You are frequently disappointed by or bitter about your love relationships.
- You marry someone who begins to resemble an ex-partner or parent you loathe.
- You have started to act "just like" the person, parent or ex-spouse you dislike.
- You find yourself experiencing the same career or money conflicts your parents had.
- You find yourself re-enacting similar dramas from a previous love relationship.
- You still regret mistakes or missed opportunities in your love life.
- You re-create in your adult life emotionally upsetting

situations similar to the unresolved incidents of your childhood (only the characters and setting have changed).
• You feel like giving up on love.
• You feel estranged, emotionally isolated.
• You believe you never received the support or love you needed to be happy and fulfilled.

Most people recognize one or more of these signs of buried emotional wounds. A primary objective of depth psychotherapy is to uncover these old hurts and painstakingly work them through to resolution. In no way do I wish to imply that the pain of such traumas can be resolved by simply reading a chapter. However, by demystifying the process of healing and understanding how these old wounds affect your current psychology, you can help resolve old emotional traumas. For the basically healthy person who is well motivated, the emotional workouts in this chapter can assist in healing resentments and discovering a deeper capacity for peace and passion.

Childhood Struggles

The quality of your parents' marriage is among the most important factors in determining the quality of your own love relationship. Most people cringe at this idea. Don't worry–you are not doomed to have a love relationship no better than your parents. Although all of us have an innate tendency to repeat our parents' mistakes, we can also avoid them. What is needed is an understanding of how your parents' relationship affected you; the negative traits you picked up and how to change them.

I have devised a list of questions designed to help you identify emotional habits or traits learned from your parents. I suggest you discuss these questions with your partner or a friend, to help you loosen the grip of a painful childhood. Take your time with each of these questions, and don't hold back. Let your feelings surface whether you are angry, sad, humiliated, enraged or embarrassed. Accepting your emotions is part of the healing process.

1. What was your parents' relationship like with each other? Was your father or mother in a dominant or submissive role? Describe the feelings, tone and behavior between your parents. Give concrete and specific incidents.

2. Were they mostly kind and loving, or were they critical and emotionally distant? What was the atmosphere like in your home when you were growing up? Was it tense, serious and bitter, or lighthearted, excited and relaxed? Was it very different at different ages? What accounted for this? Did your parents show physical affection for each other, such as hugs, kisses or intimate talks? Did you sense that your parents were covering up conflicts around money, sex, alcoholism or other issues? Be specific.

3. Over what issues did arguments arise in your family: jealousy, work, friends, values, etc.? Did you fight over dating, eating, drinking, cleanliness, household chores, schoolwork, neatness or curfew? Give examples; recount concrete incidents from your childhood and adolescence.

4. How did each of your parents treat you? Did either make degrading comments that left you feeling ashamed, humiliated or inferior? What specific statements did they make that you've never forgiven them for? Was there any emotional, physical or sexual abuse?

5. How did you deal with rejection when you felt put down, controlled or rejected? Did you get angry or have a temper tantrum? Were you withdrawn or rebellious? Did you scream and yell? Did you try harder to be a "good boy" or "nice girl"? Did you cry and feel sorry for yourself? Share specific memories.

6. In what ways are you like your mother or father? In what ways are you different from them? What specific resentments do you carry toward each of your parents? If a parent was angry and critical, do you also tend to react this way? How has your unfinished business from childhood affected your adult life? How do you act out these old patterns and power struggles? Give specific examples from your current and past love life.

These questions may provoke emotional responses that surprise you. Therefore, it is best to plan to have at least an hour of uninterrupted time. To work through all the questions you will probably need more than one sitting.

The Photohistory Exercise

Here is another exercise that you and a partner can use to identify and heal hurts from childhood. There is within everyone, no matter how adult, an inner child who still carries unresolved hurt, fear and pain. Photographs or home movies of your childhood can be helpful in discovering unresolved feelings. This exercise is much more than simply reviewing an old family album. The following instructions will help you use these photographs and home videos as a tool for self-discovery and, ultimately, self-healing.

As you review the photohistory of you or your partner, consider: What insecurities and pressures were controlling that small child? How did that child feel about himself/herself? What unresolved conflicts affected his/her moods? Were your parent(s) stern and critical, or approving and loving?

Look at the expressions of each family member–the way they sit or stand and the body language that is visible in the photographs. What pressures were on the parents' and children's shoulders? What was the relationship like between siblings? Were they competitive, supportive, loving or cold? What traumas, losses and deaths affected your family?

Home videos are also a way in which to appreciate the tradition, religion, national origin and family struggles that make an individual unique. It may be important to ask about and understand the social, political and economic forces that affected you, what it was like emigrating to another country, what it was like growing up with various hardships.

Through examining old photos with your partner, you may discover clues to negative patterns. It can be deeply healing to share with one another childhood pains–and triumphs. As Santayana said, "Those who cannot remember the past are condemned to repeat it."

The Crisis of an Affair

An affair can produce a severe crisis of mistrust and rage. This is true whether the couple is in a committed relationship or already married. Once two people have committed to a monogamous relationship, an outside affair can severely impair the love bond. One party may feel as guilty as the other feels betrayed. Unless the resentments are healed, the relationship either becomes bitter or falls apart.

Mark and Nina illustrate the challenge of overcoming an affair and rebuilding a marriage. When Nina picked up Mark from the airport after a business convention, she found him to be unusually quiet and pensive. On the drive home, he suddenly blurted out that he had had a fling with a saleswoman named Camille.

In shock, Nina immediately pulled off the road. As if to appease her, Mark said that it was just impulsive and he had practiced safe sex. He told her that she had nothing to worry about; that the whole thing was no big deal.

That night Nina felt as if her husband of ten years was a stranger. Mark kept apologizing and assuring her that it had only been a one-time thing. She felt so hurt and humiliated that she wondered whether she should walk out.

Over the next few weeks, Nina increasingly made sarcastic remarks to Mark while trying to restrain most of her anger. She developed headaches, stomach pains and insomnia. Their emotional distance grew and their sex life became non-existent. Nina felt like a "volcano about to burst" with no safe outlet.

I felt deeply for Nina's feelings of hurt, betrayal and bitterness. In counseling, I emphasized to her the importance of working through her painful resentments. If she did not release her suppressed feelings of hurt and anger, she would remain imprisoned by them.

In many love relationships, one or both partners have a tendency to bury those resentments they are afraid to face. They store memories of abuse, betrayal and rejection because they are afraid of losing the relationship. Some result from little annoyances and minor irritations that are part of daily living. Other resentments such as infidelity or physical abuse are major. In all cases, resentments fester and poison love.

Initially, Nina was so numb she was unable to confront Mark. Nina had to acknowledge her resentment and pain for the healing process to begin.

Writing the Wrong

I suggested to Nina that she set aside time to make a list of her resentments; to describe each hurt as specifically as possible. Once she started her list, tears and anger began to pour out. Here is a partial list of Nina's resentments:

"I hate you for screwing Camille."

"I hate you for your betrayal and the pain you caused me."

"I hate you for humiliating me."

"I hate you for saying 'it was just impulsive', and because it was 'safe sex' that I had nothing to worry about."

"I resent your sexist 'no big deal' attitude; if I had had a fling, you'd be crushed."

"I hate you for expecting me to be immediately understanding, when I needed to scream and cry."

"I resent you for making it sound like you're the one suffering because I'm rejecting you."

"I hate you for blaming me for the lack of passion in our sex life."

"I resent you for getting upset whenever I ask for comfort and reassurance."

"I resent you for trying to be all smiles, and for your 'everything is wonderful' attitude."

"I resent you for telling me to 'get over it' and to not be so angry."

When Nina completed the "Writing the Wrong" exercise, she felt as if a load had been lifted from her shoulders. The purpose of this exercise is not to wallow in pain but to safely release rage-filled, bitter feelings. Once you write down and release your resentments, you will be in a better position to initiate a constructive dialogue, when and if appropriate. You will be better able to share your hurt and anger effectively by first doing some psychological housecleaning.

Exorcising Rage

Earlier I discussed the difference between constructive and destructive anger. One subject I didn't yet broach is the difference between anger and rage. The difference is more than just one of degree. Anger can be a constructive energy to facilitate communication. Rage is a destructive energy, and can be an overpowering force. While anger is the natural response to ordinary hurts of love, rage is a primal reaction to betrayal, threats to survival and abuse.

Rage, characterized by the intention to destroy, must always be appropriately discharged using safe and effective means. I suggested Nina take a tennis racquet or foam bat and repeatedly hit her bed or couch. I cautioned her to be careful not to do any damage to herself or valued belongings. While Mark was at work, she closed the door to her bedroom and turned off her phone. When she began to visualize Mark with Camille, she felt a surge of rage and betrayal.

When she first began pounding her bed, she felt awkward and inhibited. Once she got into it, however, she felt a tremendous release of pent-up rage. Nina pounded the mattress with the racquet, and angrily shouted, "You bastard; you bitch; I hate you both for what you did!" Nina visualized the negative aspects of Mark as she did this. "How dare you give someone else your passion, and give me boring sex! How would you like it if I went out and had a wild affair? You selfish sleaze; I hate you!"

After about forty minutes she felt completely spent and drained. Nina had given herself permission to appropriately act-out her revenge fantasies in a fierce, but safe release. Later she commented, "My throat got sore, but after lots of yelling, I was able to cry and release my feelings of pain. I also felt lighter, and after releasing my rage, a lot more powerful."

Everyone has some suppressed feelings of rage, but usually these feelings are so powerful and unacceptable that we push them into our dark side, the shadow self. Having a safe means to release rage can give you back your vitality, self-esteem and fierceness.

The first step in healing your own rage is to acknowledge the existence of this violent energy within. Accepting this dark side of you can be frightening. To test whether you may be harboring buried rage, think back on those incidents where you may have been betrayed or abused by a friend or partner, or humiliated by a parent or teacher. If the rage is there, the memory alone may cause your jaw to clench or your heart rate to accelerate.

To release your pent-up rage safely and constructively, do the "Exorcizing Rage" workout described above. Imagine the painful incident, or the negative aspects of the person who hurt you, as you beat the mattress or couch and scream out your resentments.

Additional ways to let off steam are jogging, brisk walking, aerobics, dancing, swimming, competitive sports and other forms of vigorous exercise. Beware, however, of using sports as a means of escaping from rage. In order to release rage, you must get in touch with the memories of your injury. For example, you can play a game of tennis in which you picture the tennis ball being the negative aspects of the person you feel rage toward. Alternatively, you can hit a punching bag while you envision the painful incident.

Another important reason to discharge rage safely and appropriately is to avoid having a debilitating depression. Depression can sometimes be anger turned inward. As you express rather than depress your resentments, you can begin to truly contemplate forgiveness.

Forgiving from the Heart

Learning to forgive has been advocated by the greatest spiritual teachers. Modern psychological research confirms the importance of forgiving fully, for creating peace and passion in your love relationship. To forgive does not mean to forget, but it does mean to let go and move beyond.

Holding on to rage and resentment can cause cynicism and

bitterness to poison love. Intimacy remains clouded with venom and fear: "I still feel enraged with that rotten s.o.b.," or "I feel so angry, I still want revenge." The price of withholding forgiveness is inner peace, and an impaired capacity to love and be loved.

Early in counseling, I asked Nina, "Do you want to let go of your resentments, or do you want to extract punishment?" I explained that if she sought revenge, she could remain bitter. If she chose to forgive, the release and relief would free *her* and restore love. She wanted to be able to forgive.

I suggested the following "Forgiving from The Heart" visualization exercise:

Find a comfortable spot and make sure you will not be disturbed for thirty minutes. Close your eyes, relax and visualize you and your partner (or whomever you are working on forgiving–a parent, a friend, an ex-spouse) in an appropriate setting, perhaps your current home. If for some reason you find it difficult to visualize, try expressing your feelings while looking at a photograph of him or her.

With the image in mind, say in your own words, "Out of the love I have for you, and the love you have for me, there are some things we need to clear up, from my heart to yours." For the next twenty or so minutes, continue to visualize your love partner, and fully express the resentments you harbor. Imagine you have complete permission to say whatever is in your heart. Throughout, picture your partner giving you the receptivity, support, and respect you need.

To complete the exercise, take a few deep breaths and imagine a healing light sweeping over both of you. The light can be seen as emanating from any source comfortable to you–God, your Higher Power. Just as light can help heal a physical wound, this light can assist in healing the bitterness in your heart. Relax for five to ten minutes in this light. If you experience any irritability, be sure to take additional time to rest and let go.

After the exercise, you may feel emotionally fatigued. Lie down, take a few deep breaths and let yourself unwind. Repeat the exercise until your "heavy" resentments lose their intensity and become "lighter."

Nina found the "Forgiving from The Heart" exercise extremely powerful. As she described it, "I pictured Mark and myself sitting in our den, and all sorts of feelings came up–disgust, revulsion and sadness. For the first time I could fully express myself; I didn't have to deal with Mark's resistance or an angry tirade. After ten minutes into the visualization, I felt tears streaming down my face. I was so relieved to get the negativity out of my system." After several sessions, Nina experienced a release from resentment and a slow reopening of her heart.

A Heart Letter

If you try to deal with a recent betrayal in a Heart Talk, you may not get very far. Emotions may be too raw and volatile to attempt to reconcile. Your partner may get defensive and interrupt you. The intensity of your rage may block a constructive sharing of your feelings. One way to overcome this barrier to heart-to-heart communication is through a "Heart Letter."

In this exercise, you write down in a letter form your hurt, anger, fear and loss. When you have been emotionally wounded, there can be an overwhelming desire to take immediate action; writing a Heart Letter meets this need. Describing your emotions on paper establishes a beginning, middle and end. This helps to reduce inner chaos and gives a renewed sense of control and power. Following a Heart Letter, you will find yourself in a more positive frame of mind to elicit a meaningful Heart Talk with your partner.

To continue her healing process, I gave Nina the following instructions for writing a Heart Letter:

1. Describe the full intensity of your feelings. Beware of merely dumping accusations on your partner. Be specific about the injury and the pain.
2. Express your feelings of pain with "I" statements such as: "I felt betrayed when . . ." "I still feel unresolved about . . ." or "I am angry that . . ."
3. Take responsibility for your feelings, and avoid accusatory "you" statements such as "You did this..." or "You should've. . ."
4. Express the hope that you can both work this through and grow from the incident. Acknowledge that you've equally contributed to a breakdown in communication. The issue is not to place blame and shame upon your partner but to learn how to improve and rebuild the trust in your relationship.
5. Express love and the desire to forgive and rebuild intimacy. The Heart Letter is not complete until you have written about both forgiveness and love.
6. You don't have to pretend that you don't love your partner in order to punish him or her. In fact, the more you can express feelings of tenderness, as well as hurt, the more likely that your partner can acknowledge your pain.
7. Forgiveness doesn't mean forgetting or white-washing what has happened, but rather letting go, moving on and focusing on the positive. The reason to make peace is primarily for you, and only secondarily for your partner. It is you who will suffer if you hold on to the pain and resentment. Forgiving is "for giving" yourself peace of mind.

Allow yourself to express and work through your anger, hurt, fear and sadness until you experience a new sense of love and understanding. The process of releasing negative feelings and coming to a genuine state of love and forgiveness is essential to personal growth. When you stop loving, it is you who suffers the most. When you hold on to rage, resentment and bitterness, it is your flow of love that is blocked. When you are willing to work through your negative emotions you are the winner, for you become whole once again.

In each Heart Letter, begin by expressing your anger, and allow yourself to progress through each of the following emotional levels until you can re-access your love. The following phrases can help you move from one stage to the next:

Level 1: Anger. Express your rage, resentment and fury: "I hate it when . . .," "I am furious that . . .," "I'm disgusted with . . .," "I resent . . .," "I'm fed up with . . .," "I can't stand . . .," "I am bitter about…," "I felt violated when…"

Level 2: Hurt. Express your hurt, disappointment and pain: "It hurts me when. . .," "I feel disappointed that . . .," "I feel rejected when . . .," "I feel jealous when you . . .," "It's devastating that . . .," "I felt abandoned when…"

Level 3: Fear. Express your fear, anxiety and insecurity: "I feel scared when I . . .," "I am frightened when you . . .," "I'm afraid that . . .," "I feel tense and anxious when you . . .," "I feel insecure about . . .," "I dread…," "I felt terrified when…"

Level 4: Sadness: Express your feelings of loss, remorse and grief: "I'm sorry that . . .," "I regret that . . .," "I become tearful about…," "I feel sad that I . . .," "I feel a loss of safety…," "I feel grief over . . .," "I feel guilty because . . ."

Level 5: Wishes. Express your hopes, goals and wants: "I want us to see a therapist…," "I'd like for each of us to do a Heart Letter…," "I wish I felt . . ," "I hope . . .," "I wish you had . . .," "I want . . .," "My goals are to…"

Level 6: Love and forgiveness. Express your love,

understanding and forgiveness: "I love you because . . .," "What I love most about you is . . .," "Thanks to our relationship, I . . .," "I'm proud of you for . . .," "I forgive you for . . .," "I forgive myself for . . .," "I love it when . .," "I understand that . . .," "What I have learned is . . ."

Nina gathered her courage, followed the instructions, and composed the following Heart Letter:

Dear Mark,

Out of my love for you, and the commitment to our relationship, there are some deep feelings I need to share. I bring up this unfinished business out of the sincere desire to have completion and to be more loving. I did both of us a disservice by being so nice and understanding right after you told me about the affair. I'm glad you told me, but inside I was burning up, so I need to share all of my feelings with you.

I despise you for having the affair. It makes me sick to think of you having sex with another woman. I hate having to worry about whether or not I am in danger of having AIDS, herpes or other sexually transmitted diseases. I'm disgusted by your big, insecure, sexual ego. I hate picturing you flirting with that little bitch. I felt hatred when you asked me to put a smile on my face and forget about it. I resent you for not giving me more of an opportunity to share my anger with you.

I feel so hurt by what you did my heart is breaking. I feel disgust when I imagine you laughing and joking with Camille, while I sat home alone. I feel betrayed and deeply rejected. I feel so sad and distant from you. It hurts me that you gave so much attention to another woman, yet your sex drive with me is flat.

I'm afraid our marriage is over now. I'm afraid I'll never be able to trust you again. I'm afraid you aren't in love with me anymore. I'm scared you find other women more attractive than me, and that I'm no longer what you want. I'm scared I can't handle the competition out there. I'm afraid this affair will always come between us. I'm scared of losing you and being alone.

I'm sorry I wasn't giving you what you needed, and you went elsewhere. I'm sorry that all of this has happened. Please understand my pain. I need you to hold me, accept my feelings and make me feel special again.

I want to trust you again. I want to forgive you. I want to work through my grief. I want to have fun again. I want to heal this trauma and move on. I want us to be happy together again. I don't want to feel threatened when you go off on business. I want to love you and rekindle our passion.

I still love you,
Nina

After Mark read this Heart Letter, they talked and wept together for several hours. As Nina shared, "This was a huge breakthrough because we had been walking on eggshells ever since the affair." Mark said he felt relieved to finally talk about their relationship difficulties. They began to have hope and see light at the end of the tunnel.

A relationship crisis is not only a breakdown, but also an opportunity to break through to a new level of growth. In an intimate relationship, both people are constantly evolving as individuals and as a couple. Heart Letters, in addition to Heart Talks, are another way to communicate intimate feelings. "I love you" doesn't become pat and insincere, but remains clear, bright and honest.

Through their commitment to communicate heart to heart, Nina and Mark turned their marital crisis into an opportunity to become closer; they achieved a real breakthrough. In a follow-up session one-year later, they reported their sexual intimacy and love life had reached a completely new level of peace and passion.

As emphasized in Chapter 3, there is no innocent party in an unhappy love relationship. Each partner is one hundred percent responsible for the success of the relationship. While there was no excusing Mark's extramarital affair, it was important to understand the deeper causes.

When Nina looked back, she realized she had been denying problems in their relationship. Nina and Mark lost some of the intimacy and emotional connection that made their relationship vibrant. They allowed their lives to become so busy that there was no time for romance and intimacy.

Once Mark and Nina assumed joint responsibility for their growth, they were able to make substantial, positive changes. They each took full responsibility for creating peace and passion in the relationship.

Rx for the Hard-Hearted: Appreciation

In long-term love relationships, there is a tendency to take each other for granted and give less and less acknowledgement of your partner's good qualities, such as being warm, affectionate and considerate. Partners who take each other for granted often criticize each other for becoming hard-hearted, selfish and unfeeling. This process becomes self-fulfilling as criticism begets criticism. Part of the solution involves asking yourself, "Is this what I want in my life and in my love relationship? Is this really what I want to see happen?"

Why do relationships become unfulfilling? One reason may be that you no longer give attention to what attracted you to your partner in the first place. In fact, you may have gone so far as to focus on the unpleasant experiences you've had together, disregarding the pleasant ones you have shared. How does this happen?

You may have exaggerated images of your partner's bad habits. Perhaps you remember all the hateful things said and every hostile argument you've ever had. As these memories and images are played over and over again, resentments grow deeper and it soon becomes impossible to see any positive qualities in the person you once loved so dearly. If you only pay attention to the negative, it grows stronger in your life.

What if, in the middle of a heated argument, you chose to recall something good about your partner (e.g., you remembered your partner teaching you something, a time when your partner did something really special for you, or even the first time you passionately made love)? This could have a great impact on how you treat the person you love and the outcome of your argument.

Many problems among couples arise from a lack of appreciation for each other. Partners resort to complaining when they are denied what they really want, which is appreciation. Some people would rather leave than ask to be appreciated. They say, "I shouldn't have to ask or beg for love."

Although it may seem uncomfortable, if your partner is taking you for granted, it is your responsibility to request (not demand) the appreciation you need. The consistent expression of appreciation can revitalize a relationship that has gone stale. At first it takes practice to stop taking your partner for granted, but the rewards are well worth it. The following suggestions will allow both you and your partner to feel more appreciated:

- Spend time at the end of the day to acknowledge each other for all you have done. Take turns using the Heart Talk format: "I appreciate you for . . .," "Something I'd like to be appreciated for . . .," "The best thing about our love relationship is . . .," "Among the things I love most about you are . . ." No one ever tires of hearing how much they are loved. By telling your partner what you appreciate, you are renewing love.

- Each of us thrives on different kinds of appreciation. For example, a beautiful woman may receive frequent attention for her physical attributes, but what she may really need is acknowledgment for being competent, intelligent and effective. On the other hand, a woman who is highly successful may get enough acknowledgment for her career performance, but what she may need to hear is that the love will be there whether she succeeds or fails. A man who is constantly acknowledged for being strong and in charge may also need acknowledgment for those times when he is open, cuddly and vulnerable.

- You may have difficulty graciously accepting appreciation from your partner. You may jump in to "even the score" ("I love you, too. You're wonderful also") or brush aside compliments as undeserved. If this pattern is true for you, practice receiving and enjoying praise instead of keeping yourself love-starved. Remember, there is a simple, appropriate response to a heartfelt compliment: "Thank you."

- Appreciation is a two-way street. Expressing your gratitude will also inspire your partner to acknowledge you. Look to be more appreciative. For example, "That was an excellent dinner you made." "I like that outfit you are wearing." "Your efforts to exercise have really paid off. You look great." "You are so much fun to be with." "I really enjoy it when you sing and play the piano for me." "Our love means a great deal to me." "Having you by my side gives me such strength." "I admire how honest and straightforward you are in business." "You have an excellent memory." "Your enthusiasm is contagious." "Thank you for being such a good listener." "I love how you parent our children."

When a Therapist May Be Needed

Certainly, most of life's difficulties, challenges and even crises do not require psychotherapy. Nevertheless, professional assistance may be necessary or useful in the following instances:

- If your love relationships are repeatedly frustrating.
- If you and your partner are caught in bitter conflicts, despite working at Love Fitness.
- If you don't feel good about yourself most of the time.
- If you seek solace in alcohol, drugs or binge eating.
- If you feel perpetually stressed out, worried and fearful.
- If you and your partner have sexual problems that Heart Talks don't resolve.
- If you're in a severe crisis you can't cope with.
- If you are afraid that you may act on suicidal or violent thoughts.
- If you are increasingly depressed, emotionally isolated or socially withdrawn.

The importance of carefully choosing a licensed psychotherapist cannot be overemphasized. Most people spend more time buying a car than searching for the right psychotherapist! There is nothing mysterious about counseling, and no therapist can perform magic. Any psychotherapist, no matter how brilliant, can only assist you in discovering how *you* can solve your problems; he or she cannot solve them for you.

Seek referrals from your family physician, mental health societies and trusted friends. Visit two or three psychotherapists with the intention of determining who would be best for you. After the session, did you feel more hopeful and empowered? When making your final decision, consider the following questions:

1. Do you feel safe, comfortable and at ease with the therapist?

2. Is the therapist encouraging and empowering?
3. What is the therapist's approach to your problem including strategies, goals and length of treatment?
4. Does the therapist answer your questions and concerns directly?
5. If you are interested, is the therapist willing to see your partner?
6. After the session, did you feel more hopeful and empowered?

Depression is the most common of all psychological illnesses. Many people are unaware that low energy, lack of sexual passion, and an impaired ability to love and be loved can be a biological result of depression. Almost as painful as being depressed is being the partner of someone suffering from this disorder.

All too often, people with depression fail to seek treatment because they fear the stigma of "mental illness." This is unfortunate because depression is a highly prevalent and well-recognized medical disorder, one as treatable as diabetes or hypertension. It is treated with psychotherapy and/or anti-depressant medication. Please see my book *How to Heal Depression* (Mary Books, 2004).

Chapter 7

The New Love Contract

WHEN IT COMES TO LOVE, two halves do not make a whole. The single most damaging assumption you can make in a love relationship is that you and your partner are supposed to make each other happy. This assumption makes no more sense than if you thought you could exercise for your partner to keep him or her physically fit. Happiness arises from personal growth–developing your health, skills, achievements, capacity for intimacy, friendships, success, peace of mind, values and spirituality. A healthy love relationship and family life can add enormously to that growth. However, if you abdicate responsibility for your own happiness, problems in your love relationship are inevitable.

Becoming Fit for Love Together

You may acknowledge intellectually that you can't expect someone else to make you happy, but the challenge is taking this concept to heart. How do you acknowledge your needs without becoming needy? Is your self-esteem excessively dependent on your partner's approval or feelings toward you? How do you develop and express yourself without being a threat to your partner? How do you handle your own stress and frustration without succumbing to the tendency to blame? How do you get what you want from a relationship without being caught in self-defeating efforts to try to change your partner? The answer lies in consciously creating a new love contract.

By love "contract," I am not referring to a legal written document. Rather, I mean the spoken and unspoken psychological promises partners make to one another. In the business world, conflict arises when people make promises they can't keep. They wind up breaching their contract.

So, too, love partners sometimes make emotional promises they can't keep. When partners unconsciously enter into an unspoken agreement that each look to the other as the primary source of personal happiness, they make a psychological promise they are bound to breach.

It is easy to understand how and why partners wind up assuming that each should be responsible for the other's happiness. Partners naturally want to please each other and to earn each other's approval. Out of mutual commitment to each other, partners desire to meet each other's needs.

Living together involves some divisions of labor, whether one person cares for the home and the other works outside the home, or whether all these duties are shared. This sharing of lives together encourages a feeling of responsibility for your partner's well-being and happiness.

While all these reasons explain how partners assume each is responsible for the other's happiness, a simple fact remains: Personal happiness depends on your own personal growth, not on your partner.

The Old-Style Love Contract: Co-Dependency

The underlying assumption of the old-style love contract is, "I am responsible for your happiness and you are responsible for mine." You might think, "Of course, that is what love is all about." A more careful examination reveals how the old-style contract gets emotionally played out.

Since happiness stems from within, a relationship based on the old-style love contract usually winds up with partners feeling disappointed with each other. How couples handle a major business failure or economic setback typically illustrates the problem. When financial disaster hits, one partner may try to be understanding but secretly feels let down. A protracted illness can also highlight the problem. When one partner isn't there for the other, resentments may grow in the caregiver behind a facade of tenderness.

More commonly, when you feel bored, moody or frustrated, you may be expecting your partner to magically boost your spirits. Unfortunately, no matter what your partner has to offer, his or her attempts are eventually doomed to failure. What then follows is a tirade of complaints and blame such as, "My life would be terrific if you would . . . [do what I say, take care of household chores, lose weight, stop spending so much money, etc.]."

Such co-dependency can also inhibit you from pursing your own goals. Couples caught in the old-style love contract tend to allow one partner to pursue personal achievement while the other assumes a supporting role. For some couples, this arrangement works wonderfully. For many others, however, time passes, children grow up, and the caregiver, who may now feel unfulfilled careerwise, resents having passed up the earlier opportunity to pursue his or her dreams. Even when both partners work, it often happens that one will take a "safe job" so the other can pursue his or her dreams. The one who fails to reach for his or her personal star may wind up feeling frustrated and resentful.

Taking unreasonable responsibility for your partner's moods also results in unnecessary guilt and worry. If you believe you are responsible for your partner's happiness, you feel guilty about his or her frustration and worry that the cause is somehow your fault. Unfortunately, no matter how much you try to help or please, you cannot make your partner be happy.

Though every person must ultimately take responsibility for his or her own happiness, it is quite natural to wish for a magical partner who can do it all for you. Perhaps you fantasized that a Prince or a Princess would come along to give you the romantic bliss you were craving. Romantic infatuation can be so glorious that even the most ordinarily sensible person can be heard to say, "I have finally found the one who can make me happy." Unfortunately, when the infatuation wears off, you begin to wonder if you found the right person after all. Romantic illusions inevitably lead to anger and disappointment.

Love Fitness requires letting go of the assumption that someone else can make you happy. Instead, you must commit to choosing satisfaction in your own life, and in your love relationship, on a moment-to-moment basis. The more you resist choosing satisfaction, the more likely that blaming and complaining will grow.

A high-quality love relationship is not made up of half-complete partners trying to rescue each other or trying to become whole by merging. Only when both partners are striving to be full and complete within themselves can love and happiness overflow.

Choosing to be satisfied doesn't mean that you settle for less or become complacent. Rather, it means that you look for concrete ways to develop your aspirations in harmony with those of your partner. There will always be challenges to balancing individual happiness with maintaining relationship harmony. What if you desire children at different times? What if you get important career opportunities in different cities? What if one of you wants to go back to school? These issues will challenge you, and Heart Talks can provide help.

Taking responsibility for your own happiness is learning to soothe and support yourself when fears and doubts arise. How often have you used fears, or a victimized facial expression, to induce your partner to make critical decisions for you? How often have you pretended you couldn't face an issue when in fact you could have, but didn't want to? How often have you waited for external forces to make your decisions for you? Though you may know that you are responsible for your choices and that you cannot abdicate that responsibility to your partner, the key is acting on that awareness, in all your affairs.

Exploring Your Love Contract: A Quiz

The following quiz is intended to help you assess the degree to which you take responsibility for your own happiness and choices in your love relationship. Read each of the thirty-three statements as if you were speaking to your partner (or, if you are not currently in a relationship, the person with whom you last had an intimate involvement). On reading each of the statements below, ask yourself whether it applies to you rarely, sometimes, often or always. Score 3 for rarely, 2 for sometimes, 1 for often, and 0 for usually.

1. I struggle to be more of an individual person in our relationship.
2. I try to guess what you need and feel frustrated when I am wrong.
3. I expect you to know what I want, and to give it to me unflinchingly.
4. I feel guilty saying no to your requests for fear of making

you unhappy.

5. When I want something from you, I feel hurt when you say no.
6. I don't feel happy unless you are also happy.
7. I feel I cannot live without you.
8. I feel guilty if you are not sexually satisfied.
9. I feel used, rather than loved and appreciated.
10. I feel pressured by your wishes and desires.
11. I feel you expect me to make you happy.
12. I feel blamed by you when things go wrong.
13. I blame myself for our problems.
14. I am afraid I can't trust you.
15. I regret giving up my personal goals for your career and raising our family.
16. I want you to make me happy.
17. I hold back expressing myself around you.
18. I try to rescue you from experiencing any difficulties.
19. I feel love can solve all problems.
20. I don't need family/friends; I need you.
21. I feel I have to be strong and responsible so you won't feel scared or disappointed.
22. I feel guilty when you are unhappy.
23. I fear you won't stay if you need me less.
24. I feel selfish if I pursue my own happiness and desires.
25. I am afraid I will not be sexually satisfied.
26. I fear you will outgrow the relationship and leave me.
27. I have to give up my desires in order to please you.
28. I need to protect, defend and save you.
29. I feel that our love is a prison; I've lost my freedom and happiness.
30. I count on you to make my major decisions when I don't know what to do.
31. If you loved me, you would do what I say.
32. I fear being economically dependent on you.

33. I feel responsible when you feel hurt or upset.

Now add up your total score to assess the level of freedom and personal autonomy you experience in the relationship:

80-99 You experience an abundance of freedom in your relationship. You are a whole individual who enjoys interdependence and understands that the source of personal happiness lies within.

60-79 You enjoy above average autonomy in your love relationship. You know how to meet your needs and don't make your partner responsible for your personal satisfaction.

40-59 Although you have enough independence to hold your own in a relationship, you may often feel "If you really loved me, you would . . . ," causing you conflict and unnecessary frustration.

20-39 You are too emotionally dependent and look to the relationship to make you happy. The expectations upon your partner may be excessive or demanding.

0-19 You blame your partner for your frustrations and unhappiness.

Pay particular attention to statements on which you scored 0 or 1, and ask yourself how these attitudes and beliefs affect you and your relationship. If possible, have your partner complete this quiz as well. When reviewing the results together, beware: Don't use the quiz to blame, but rather to learn. Be sure to acknowledge yourself and your partner for the courage and commitment it takes to explore your love contract.

False Assumptions

One terribly destructive offshoot of assuming that you are responsible for your partner's happiness is believing that love is a license to change your partner. What usually lies behind such efforts is a desire to make your partner fit your unrealistic expectations and false assumptions. Below are two case examples:

1. Melanie and Bradley lived together for three years. Although Melanie wanted to get married, Bradley kept putting it off because he wasn't "ready." The more Bradley resisted a commitment, the more Melanie coaxed him to "overcome his fears and grow up." Melanie had often spent her energy trying to "fix" unavailable, uncommitted men. She found unstable partners to be challenging, unpredictable ones to be mysterious, immature ones to be demanding–and all of them in need of her psychological support. When asked about her suggestions, Bradley declared, "Melanie is always trying to 'help' me be more intimate, but that just makes me feel like running away."

By assuming the role of "therapeutic rescuer," Melanie was trying to force Bradley into filling her expectations of the perfect partner. Melanie also had the expectation that "in the end" she would be deeply appreciated for her efforts. What she had to recognize is that no man wants to feel scrutinized and badgered. Her efforts to understand and "enlighten" him were actually manipulative and controlling. Through counseling, Melanie discovered that this desire to "help" was really an effort to force Bradley to provide the perfect, romantic love she so desperately sought. Melanie had to learn to accept a man as he is, not as she hoped he would be. Only by giving up the need to control could she accept her partner as he is.

2. After a six-month whirlwind romance during which Dana, a professional chef, often prepared gourmet meals that took days to plan, Matthew, a stockbroker, proposed to the only woman who, he said, "cooks better than Mom!" Yet nine months into marriage, Matthew was seriously troubled by Dana's new "attitude." "Things were better before we got married. Dana used to take such good care of me, but now she never has time,"

he lamented. Dana, on the other hand, felt Matthew was too demanding and jealous of her friends and activities.

Like so many men, Matthew confused love from his wife with motherly love–which comes only once in a lifetime. He sought from Dana the special quality of nurturance he had received from his mother. This included fixing all his meals, cleaning up after him and just generally indulging him. When Matthew began berating Dana for not being more caring, Dana eventually blew up.

Through counseling, Matthew saw that he was expecting Dana to be his "super mom" because he was still tied to his mother's apron strings. Matthew had to stop trying to force Dana into a mother/child role and to instead join her in creating an adult/adult love relationship. In time, Matthew and Dana learned to function as true partners.

A paradox of unconditional love is recognizing that we all have conditions. No relationship is "perfect." The more you accept that no partner will ever fit all your pictures, the more you can appreciate the partner you've chosen to be with. A relationship isn't your salvation, your experience of love, joy and satisfaction will always rest primarily within you.

You must give yourself the freedom to be exactly who you are. You don't owe it to your partner to be anyone other than who you truly are. With this attitude about yourself, you empower your partner to also be authentic.

Beyond the Blame Game

When you were a young child, the responsibility for your happiness rested with your parents. An infant cannot feed, comfort or clothe itself. A small child cannot survive, physically or emotionally, without the consistent help of others. Because of such dependency, you learned to behave in ways that would get others to do what you could not do for yourself. You discovered how to cry when you were hungry, and to throw a temper tantrum when you didn't get your way.

As adults, we retain basic psychological needs for affection, support and nurturance. Many people assume that the responsibility for satisfying these needs is still outside of them, still primarily up to others. When we feel frustrated at work, we blame our boss or office politics. When we see a character trait in ourselves we don't like, we blame it on our parent(s). When we get bored or are in a lousy mood, we can always blame our partner.

Your partner is the most convenient person to blame for your flaws, failures and flops. How often have you shrugged your shoulders, pouted or complained, in order to manipulate your partner into doing something you could have just as well done for yourself? ("Where's the butter?" or "I can't find my pants.") How often have you blamed your love partner for your own shortcomings? ("How could you pig out in front of me when I'm trying to lose weight?" or "Why can't you make the kids respect me more?") How often have you told your partner to make a decision for both of you and then complained about the outcome? ("Why did you pick this lousy movie?" or "This Chinese restaurant is awful.")

Blaming and complaining are insidious emotional traps. It is so easy, almost natural, to blame your partner for your own problems and failures. Some people unload personal frustrations on whoever is nearest and dearest. Blaming and complaining is the adult version of the whining child. You act like the "poor me" martyr, complete with tears, tantrums and threats.

Twenty-six-year-old Jane runs a small business out of her home in the country, while her husband Keith is a lawyer in a neighboring town. Jane and Keith each had a long list of complaints that threatened to end their marriage. Jane said, "I have no time for myself. I work on my business at home and take care of the three children. I feel I have nothing exciting to get up for in the morning." Keith declared, "When I get home from seeing clients, Jane is miserable, the kids need my attention, and I feel completely neglected. If this is all marriage is, let me off at the next stop."

Jane felt that Keith had no empathy for her and the pressures she faced daily. Even though Keith did help out with the children while she worked in the home office, she felt he did so resentfully. She complained about the odd jobs around the house that Keith put off completing. Consequently, Jane began to resent giving Keith attention, and instead felt upset with him most of the time. She lamented, "I hate being a nag, but Keith doesn't help the situation."

Keith felt agitated because Jane did not appreciate that he took care of the children in the evenings, while she was working. He cooked dinner, tucked them into bed, and tidied up the house. Keith resented that Jane paid more attention to what he didn't do, rather than acknowledge all the responsibilities he assumed around the house. As a result, Keith found himself seething with anger and making sharp, derisive comments.

In a love relationship that deteriorates into blaming and complaining, each partner feels like "poor me." Rather than work through the challenges of their situation, Keith and Jane would resort to emotional weapons to manipulate each other. Each would attack by sulking, yelling and withdrawing love.

Here is the "Blaming and Complaining" exercise I gave to Keith and Jane to break the vicious cycle. Each was asked to list on a sheet of paper specific complaints about the other. I then showed them how remarkably polarized their blaming and complaining had become, when compared numerically point-by-point:

Jane

1. You always want things your way.
2. You are so predictable and compulsive. You don't take

time for fun.
3. You are always worrying about business and money.
4. You are too secretive.
5. You are too insensitive.
6. You are so opinionated; you can never be wrong.
7. You always interrupt and never let me talk.
8. You are so macho.
9. You act like a loner or stranger to me.
10. You are emotionally as tight as a clam.

Keith

1. You never make decisions.
2. You are too impulsive, outrageous and silly. You always want to play.
3. You don't think about how much you spend.
4. You pry too much.
5. You are overly emotional.
6. You are too nice; easily influenced by friends.
7. You withdraw and punish me with cold silence.
8. You are too needy.
9. You don't respect my need for space and privacy.
10. You just want to talk about your feelings; not mine.

This "Blaming and Complaining" exercise was useful in three respects. First, it helped to get their frustrations out in the open. Second, it demonstrated how stuck they were in either-or thinking. Third, this exercise showed how each was failing to acknowledge the other's point of view. They matched each other point-for-point in the blaming and complaining game, but they weren't resolving their problems. Fortunately, Shane and Keith shared the love and motivation to put into practice the following solutions:

The 200 Percent Relationship

Love fitness requires taking full responsibility for your choices, thoughts and feelings. Many people agree with taking personal responsibility–until they are in an argument. Then they resort to blaming their partner and finding fault.

Old-style relationship contracts were a 50-50 division of responsibility; new-style love contracts are 100-100. Rather than feel victimized and miserable, each partner must take 100 percent responsibility for the results in their relationship, including any problems created and finding their solutions. If you and your partner can each make such a commitment, you can enjoy a 200 percent relationship.

From this 200 percent perspective, the next time your partner is upset, ask yourself the following questions:

1. What is the reason my partner has for thinking, feeling and behaving this way?
2. What am I doing to elicit, provoke or maintain my partner's distress?
3. What experiences or assumptions underlie my feelings of being hurt, threatened or irritated?
4. What care and compassion is my partner really seeking through his or her distress?
5. How might I choose to react to elicit a positive response from my partner?
6. What can I say to validate and acknowledge my partner?
7. What can I do right now to convey more love, understanding and acceptance to my partner?

What these questions boil down to is quite simple. Whenever you and your partner feel hurt, angry or irritated, ask, "How can I create more love, acceptance and appreciation, right now?" Shifting your attention from nagging to giving acknowledgment is a relationship-transforming skill.

Even more painful than a tirade of criticism and complaints is suppressed love. You can break through years of negativity and conflict by honoring your highest intention to love. Don't be afraid to say, "I love you," no matter how many times you may have suppressed these words in the past. Keep in mind that arguments are a signal your partner needs more care and understanding from you. Be willing to be the first to give a warm hug, instead of waiting for your partner to take the first step. It may feel awkward and risky, but the rewards for both of you can be enormous.

Rephrasing with Love

Here is a Love Fitness exercise, "Rephrasing with Love," to help shift from blaming and complaining to acknowledgement and intimacy. You can rephrase a complaint into a caring statement, and a greater opportunity for love. The key is to describe the problem in terms of your own behavior. This is the exact opposite of blaming, because you identify what you can and will do to make the relationship better. Blaming and complaining is experienced by your partner as a personal attack. It makes him or her defensive, closes down communication and thwarts intimacy. The following emotional workout, which I suggested to Jane and Keith, will offer more insight into this process. Below left is a list of blaming and complaining statements; below right is how the statements can be rephrased with love.

Blaming and Complaining vs. Rephrasing with Love

Blaming and Complaining

1. You never give me credit for how hard I work to support our lifestyle.

2. You never do anything with the kids; you're tired and don't have any time for me.

3. You yell and bitch when you come home at night; you're always so stressed out.

4. Why don't you ever create a romantic, adventurous weekend with me? I'm always the one to plan them.

5. How could you be so stupid? It's your fault! If you listened to me, these problems would never happen.

6. You're always breathing down my neck and finding fault; quit telling me how to run my life.

7. You let yourself get overweight and out of shape and don't care about looking good for me.

Rephrasing with Love

1. Sweetheart, I've had a rough day and when you have time, I need a hug and support.

2. The kids really enjoyed going with you to dinner and a movie last week. It would be great if you spent special time with them this weekend.

3. Sweetheart, when you get home, why don't you take 15 minutes alone to relax and unwind?

4. I really love it when you create excitement in our love life, like the time you (specific example). Let's do it again, honey, real soon.

5. I need to be more assertive in making our major decisions. I never again want to say, "I told you so."

6. I have a right to make my own decisions. I value your input greatly, but even if you disagree with my final decision, please accept my choices.

7. Let's start going to the gym together to get back into shape.

Try this exercise yourself. Make an uncensored list of the five biggest complaints you have about your partner. Then take each complaint and rephrase it with love. Rephrasing with Love is not just for your partner, but for you: your personal power, effectiveness and evolution in love.

Transforming Expectations into Preferences

As you take responsibility for developing Love Fitness, you will be less likely to expect the impossible from your partner. Nevertheless, you may already be carrying unrealistic expectations that cause unnecessary dissatisfaction in your love relationship. If your parents constantly put you down and nagged you, you may be intolerant of your partner criticizing you at all. If an ex-lover catered to your every whim, you might be expecting your current love partner to live up to that "sugar daddy" standard.

Some expectations, of course, are appropriate. If your partner abuses alcohol or drugs, has a history of infidelity, or is unable to make a living, you are right to be cautious and set limits.

Many expectations can be converted into preferences. I define an expectation as something you need from your partner in order to feel happy, secure and whole. In contrast, a preference may be defined as something you would prefer, but your happiness and well-being don't depend on it. Make an honest evaluation of which of the following expectations you may harbor:

"If you loved me you would . . ."
• like my friends and want to socialize with them.
• make family priorities more important than work.
• include me in all your activities.
• do what I want.
• want what I want.

- lose weight and stay in shape.
- stop watching TV when I'm trying to talk to you.
- make more money.
- be more affectionate and attentive.
- be the first to make up when we argue.
- do all the things around the house I don't like to.
- make an extra effort to make me happy.
- stop being friends with people I don't care for.
- make sacrifices for my parents and family.

Now review the statements you have checked and consider the following questions:

1. What additional expectations do you have that are not on the list?
2. How realistic are your expectations?
3. Why are these expectations important to you?
4. What could you do to impose fewer expectations on your partner?
5. What could you do to convert your heavy expectations into lighter preferences?

It is important to recognize that no partner could possibly live up to most of your expectations. Even if your partner complies with your demands, they may do so resentfully. As you develop yourself, there is less of a need to make unrealistic demands or to try to control your partner.

Even when expectations are appropriate, it is helpful to express them as "I would prefer it if you would . . . stay in shape, be more affectionate, etc." Remember, it is easier for your love partner to respond with enthusiasm to a request than to comply resentfully to a demand.

"A Spirited Afterword"
by Rev. Dr. Janine H. Burns

As the title of this book suggests, your love relationship may have at times struggled with conflict instead of peace, and apathy rather than passion. You are not alone. Unfortunately, most couples come to feel an overall dissatisfaction in their love relationship and that is why half of all marriages fail.

There is a vital missing ingredient: for a love relationship to remain passionate, enthusiasm must prevail. Enthusiasm derives from the Greek root "en-theos," to be filled with Spirit. The life of the Spirit is integral to creating peace and passion in your love relationship.

When referring to "Spirit" or "God," I mean the invisible essence, that divine energy that flows in all, through all. It doesn't matter what it is called: God, Jehovah, Allah, Buddha, Power, Spirit, Love, and Mind–it still refers to the Supreme Creative Intelligence pervading all creation.

Love Fitness must include Spirit. The term Spiritual Fitness appears to be an oxymoron. It juxtaposes that which is unbounded, Spirit, with Fitness, a word that implies discipline and focus. All the great spiritual teachers, however, spoke of the necessity of not only experiencing God's love, but of also putting it into action.

When you and your love partner share a spiritual purpose, your problems become possibilities, and your tribulations become a trail back to the love of God. The height of Spiritual Fitness is to experience Namastè, when "the God-in-me consciously honors and connects with the God-in-you."

As a minister and spiritual coach, I have been blessed to work with many couples searching to create more peace and passion in their love relationships. I will focus here on overcoming the spiritual barriers to keeping peace and passion fully alive.

During the soul's journey through life, the ego flairs up. The e.g.o. can "edge God out," creating the illusion of a separate identity from Spirit. Everybody has an ego, which is quite useful actually, when you are in a body. But when it runs the show, it disconnects us from God, because all it can think about is its own survival. By survival, I mean not just your physical existence, but also the emotional survival of your ego, the self-concept with which you identify.

When we become so identified with our attitudes, perceptions and judgments, anything that contradicts them can feel like a threat to our emotional survival. As a result, we can become more attached to being right than being happy! We fight and argue as if our life depended on it. The answer is to reconnect with Spirit; where ego was, there shall Spirit reign.

Another spiritual challenge I've observed comes from the attitude that many partners take as they enter into a love relationship. They mistakenly believe that the main reason for a committed love relationship (or marriage) is to fulfill and satisfy each other's needs. When your needs go unmet, however, you become angry and resentful. You then complain and criticize, placing the blame on your partner. You and you alone, however, are responsible for your happiness and fulfillment. A relationship is an opportunity to give from the fullness of Spirit.

A further difficulty for many couples is the lack of commitment to their relationship when things get rough or major disagreements surface. There seems to be too prevalent a mind-set of "I'll give it my best shot and if it doesn't work, I can always get a divorce." You must work through the tough times in order to enjoy an enduring, meaningful relationship. Your commitment offers the safety and protection necessary for settling any disputes and for dealing with the trials and tribulations of life. When you are committed to God, as well as to each other, relationship trials and tribulations are part of a pilgrimage to peace.

The Peace and Power of Prayer

It may *appear* that God is far away or even absent from your life. That simply is not the Truth. Spirituality is about your relationship with the Presence, Power and Love within–the God of your understanding.

Prayer, contemplation and meditation are time-tested means to consciously connect to Spirit. You have the capacity to unify with Spirit to receive inspiration, divine wisdom and love. As the thirteenth-century Christian mystic Mechthild of Magdeburg reflected: "Prayer draws down the great God into the little heart; it drives the hungry soul up into the fullness of God. It brings together two lovers, God and the soul, in a wondrous place, where they speak much of love."

Opening up to prayer begins with shifting our attention from doing to being. It's stepping away from the "busy-ness" of the day to deeply relax mind and body. Use a meditation or breathing exercise to settle down. As the bible teaches, "be still and know that I am God." As you let go of the preoccupations of the ego, you open up to a greater influx of Spirit. You transcend separation and can re-experience a deep abiding sense of unity and oneness.

Prayer is a means to connect to the God of your understanding. Some people prefer formal prayers to help heal their love relationship. If so, consider using one of the following, drawn from the world religions.

Buddhism: "May we be free of suffering. May we have happiness and contentment. May we be peaceful and at ease. May we be free. May we abide in the great innate peace."

Judaism: "Help us, oh God, to lie down in peace, and awaken us to life on the morrow. May we always be guided by your good counsel, and thus find shelter in your tent of peace."

Native American: "Give us the wisdom to love, to respect, and to be kind to one another, so that we may grow in peace of mind."

Christianity (St. Frances of Assisi): "Lord, make me an instrument of your peace. Where there is hatred, let me sow love; where there is injury, let me sow pardon; where there is doubt, faith; where there is despair, hope; where there is darkness, light; where there is sadness, joy."

Islam: "Guide us, oh God, on the path of perfect harmony, the path of those whom you have blessed with the gifts of peace, joy, serenity, and delight."

Prayers such as these recited silently or aloud, by you alone or with your partner, can aid your healing journey from conflict to peace. "Active Prayer" is a powerful tool to spiritually support you and your partner. The prayer is "Active" because it is made to a God that is not only almighty and above you but expresses in you, through you and as you. This style of praying shifts the responsibility from the creator to you co-creating with God.

An "Active Prayer" is positive, affirmative and made in the present tense. Even if what you are contemplating is not currently true for you, remember you are unifying with Spirit to co-create and invoke the experience. What you believe creates your reality. "Active Prayer" recognizes that in reality, authentic inner change is made by you, in concert with the God of your understanding.

This doesn't mean you are not profoundly grateful for blessings and Divine Grace. What it does mean is that you are actively responsible for your own life. Active Prayer affirms that God is within you and around you, and therefore is completely compatible with your or any faith. Active prayer is a vehicle for you to consciously choose to live in Spirit, your most real, authentic nature. Therefore, Active Prayer is a means to live in the glory of God, and the Light of Universal love, right here, right now.

Consider using the Active Prayers that follow to help you to create peace and passion in your relationship:

Centering in Love

Today I contemplate Love.

God is Love and Love is Spirit in action.

Love is the Power within me that heals me,

protects me and guides me.

It is a Love that will never leave me nor forsake me,

a Love that is Infinite and everywhere present.

Love desires my highest good

and perfects everything that concerns me.

Love comforts me. Love forgives me.

Love inspires me. Love restores my soul.

Love is the answer to my every need.

As I contemplate Love,

it flows forth into my life and affairs,

and every moment is blessed.

I choose to reflect Love,

and I choose to express Love,

for I am centered in Love.

And so it is! Amen.

I Am Committed To My Relationship

The radiance of Spirit envelops me.

I am one with my partner in the unity of love.

When I look into my partner's eyes,

I see divine love reflected back to me.

I am totally committed to my relationship,

in sickness or in health, in good times or otherwise.

I trust in our love, even if I should feel uncertain.

I have faith in our relationship

and I repudiate any thoughts of doubt.

I am loyal to my partner and my partner is loyal to me.

I am faithful with my words and actions.

I look for the good in my partner and I praise it.

I am kind and encouraging

with my thoughts, words and actions.

I am open, sincere and authentic in my communications.

I am truthful, and I speak the truth with love.

I give my partner the freedom and space

to be a unique individual, to grow and fully express.

I am secure in my relationship,

for the Love of Spirit

protects and provides for us abundantly.

And so it is! Amen.

Releasing the Past

I am set free, I am at peace.

Yesterday is gone.

Tomorrow with its great potential is yet unborn.

There is only today in which to live fully.

I choose to live in the now.

The power of Spirit-in-me

creates my world according to my thinking.

Today, I choose to focus upon peace.

I allow thoughts of peace

to fill my mind and heart, and uplift my soul.

The problems of today now become

my opportunities for growth.

I choose to release and let go of those negative thoughts,

which bind me to the past.

I forgive anyone towards whom I have held resentment.

I release any negativity associated with that person.

I let go of any feelings of bitterness,

betrayal and resentment.

This sets me free, and allows me to be at peace.

I experience a rebirth

of freedom and harmony in my being.

There is a new enthusiasm in all I do.

I allow the Love of Spirit within me

to cleanse my mind and heart, and uplift my soul.

I am set free, I am at peace.

And so it is! Amen.

I Am Open and Receptive to Love

Love is the divine pattern within me
and everywhere present in all life.
I now free myself from all thoughts and beliefs
that are unlike this divine pattern of Love.
I willingly release and let go
of any feelings of guilt, inadequacy and fear.
I accept a wonderful, rewarding, fulfilling life experience.
I trust the Infinite Wisdom of Spirit within me
to come forth into my life and affairs,
and to create harmony and wholeness.
I am secure knowing that Spirit-in-me
brings me divine ideas for self-actualization.
The Law of Mind irresistibly attracts to me
the people and circumstances necessary
to bring forth greater peace and passion into my life.
I pay attention to my inner guidance system, my intuition.
I am open and receptive to new ideas
and wonderful opportunities that bring
peace, joy and love to myself and my love partner.
And so it is! Amen.

Remember, you can use the Power of Spirit within you to create peace and passion in your love relationship.

The Reverend Dr. Janine H. Burns holds Doctorates of Religious Studies and Divinity from Emerson Institute. As the Director of the *Guiding Light Foundation,* she is a much-sought-after speaker, spiritual coach, minister and corporate chaplain. Dr. Burns gives inspirational programs nationwide providing tools for spiritual sustenance, strength and empowerment. She serves as International Liaison for Emerson Institute. You may contact Dr. Burns c/o G.L.F., Box 472, Woodbury, N.Y. 11797.

REFERENCES

Bloomfield, Harold H., and Philip Goldberg. *Making Peace with God.* New York: PenguinPutnam, 2003.

Bloomfield, Harold H., with Philip Goldberg. *Making Peace with Your Past.* New York: HarperCollins, 2000.

Bloomfield, Harold H., with Leonard Felder. *Making Peace with Yourself.* New York: Random House, 1985.

Bloomfield, Harold H., with Leonard Felder. *Making Peace with Your Parents.* New York: Random House, 1983.

Bloomfield, Harold H., with Robert B. Kory. *Making Peace in Your Stepfamily.* Vista, CA: Peace Publishing, 2004.

Bloomfield, Harold H. *Creating a Joyful Life.* Vista, CA: Peace Publishing, 2005.

Bloomfield, Harold H., Melba Colgrove, and Peter McWilliams. *How to Survive the Loss of a Love.* Allen Park, MI: Mary Books, 2004.

Bloomfield, Harold H., and Peter McWilliams. *How to Heal Depression.* Allen Park, MI: Mary Books, 2004.

Lazarus, Arnold. *Marital Myths.* San Luis Obispo, California: Impact, 1985.

Rogers, Carl. *Becoming Partners.* New York: Delacorte, 1973.

Spiller, Jan. *Cosmic Love.* New York: Bantam, 2005.

Acknowledgements

My deep gratitude to the Rev. Dr. Janine H. Burns for her support, encouragement and brilliant editorial input in creating this updated edition. As my spiritual coach, you held my feet to the fire when needed. I thank you for being so committed to the vision for this book.

My thanks to Sirah Vettese, Ph.D., and Robert Kory, my co-authors for the early edition, entitled *Lifemates: the Love Fitness Program for a Lasting Relationship.*

Much appreciation and love to my children, Shazara, Damien and Michael. My mother Fridl, now ninety-five years old, taught me that discipline is not only a key to success, but to longevity. Nora and Gus Stern, my sister and brother-in-law, have provided me with unconditional love and incredible support.

I wish to thank Rustin Berlow, Bobby Colomby, Jimmy Dezen, Barry and Heather Dennis, Donna Lee and Larry Dennis, Carol Duncan, Phil Goldberg, Christel and Diad Hammad, Ayman Sawaf, and Maria Tonello. My love and appreciation to Jan Spiller.

I want to acknowledge my friend and this book's distributor, Van Hill, who suggested this updated edition; this project would not be possible without you. Thanks to Sandra Swift for typing the manuscript and to Michelle Goodman and Jan Keeling for their editorial services.

Special thanks to my readers for allowing me the privilege of supporting their personal and relationship growth. First and finally, my thanks to God for this opportunity. Namastè.

About HAROLD H. BLOOMFIELD, M.D.

For over thirty years, Harold H. Bloomfield, M.D., has been a leading light in the personal growth and spiritual development movements. He is a Yale-trained, award-winning psychological educator, and the author of numerous *N.Y. Times* bestselling books. Dr. Bloomfield has led millions of people to integrative healing, emotional literacy and quintessential peace.

Dr. Bloomfield's books have sold over 8 million copies worldwide and have been translated into 34 languages. How to *Survive the Loss of a Love* and *How to Heal Depression* have become self-help classics. Dr. Bloomfield's bestsellers, *Hypericum (Saint John's Wort) & Depression and Healing Anxiety Naturally* helped spur the natural medicine revolution. *TM: Discovering Inner Energy and Overcoming Stress* spent 6 months on the *New York Times* bestsellers list. His books *Making Peace with Your Parents, Making Peace with Yourself, Making Peace in Your Stepfamily, Making Peace with Your Past* and *Making Peace with God* introduced personal and family peacemaking to millions of people.

Dr. Bloomfield has appeared numerous times on Oprah, ABC's 20/20, Good Morning America, Larry King, and CNN. His work has been featured in the *New York Times, Los Angeles Times, USA Today, Time, Newsweek, Forbes, U.S. News & World Report, People, Cosmopolitan, Ladies Home Journal, Health* and *Prevention.*

Dr. Bloomfield has received the Theodore Geisel "Best of the Best" Book Award, the *Medical Self-Care Magazine* Book of the Year Award, the Golden Apple Award for Outstanding Psychological Educator and the American Holistic Health Association's Lifetime Achievement Award.